Forever Turn
The Midnight Carousel

Poems and Short Stories

Matthew Abuelo

Plain View Press
http://plainviewpress.net

1101 W 34th Street, STE 404
Austin, TX 78756

ISBN: 978-1-63210-035-1
Library of Congress Control Number: 2018933289

Cover art by Desmond Ambrose Root
Book design by Pam Knight

Other collections by Matthew Abuelo:
Organic Hotels © 2008 ISBN: 978-0-615-16898-2, Lulu.com
Last American Roar © 2006 ISBN: 978-1-4116-6382-4, Lulu.com

Other Books By This Author

The News Factory
Plain View Press-2012

Organic Hotels
Lulu.com-2009

Last American Roar
Lulu.com-2007

for Merry Becker

1963 - 2009

in memoriam

Contents

"We are all in the gutter, but some of us are looking at the stars."

Oscar Wilde

Forward

Mathew Abuelo has chosen a hard and less travelled path in his new compilation of poems and stories *Forever Turn the Midnight Carousel*. It begins in the sewers and water tunnels of New York, crawls up through rat infested subway platforms, and finally reaches a surface revealing the grim underbelly of a city in pain, slowly disintegrating into a desolate mire. He brutally tears open that underbelly and spills out a New York that we all know exists, but choose not to see; the broken, the homeless, the suicidal, the sick, the hungry, the angry, the unstable, the corrupt, those who've given up hope yet still survive, and those for whom pain summons their exit plan. Matthew Abuelo walks among them, absorbs their pain, anguish, and fear, and exorcises them in an astonishing combination of poetry and prose in interwoven language and style, resulting in a dazzling form of expression, painting pictures so vivid and alive that the city seems to bleed on his pages.

Letters to love lost in hospitals, mental wards, SROs, to drugs, depression, and suicide. Rants against greedy landlords, corrupt politicians, bad cops, uncaring social services, betrayal by friends or lovers, and the myriad of daily daggers plunged into the hearts of those least able to defend themselves. He is their voice.

His city lacks light, is musty, stagnant, dangerous, and devoid of clean air, beauty, or any compelling reason to remain. These vanquished citizens, lacking lifelines or survival skills, seem doomed to eviction, expulsion, exploitation, and slow erosion of the soul, until their options are reduced to heavy self-medication or suicide. The despair in his vision is overwhelming and cries for help, mercy, sympathy, or even just a moment of kindness. These downtrodden denizens of the city seem doomed and Abuelo pleads for a lifeline, a rescue, a change of heart; anything that might offer a glimmer of hope for a city darkened by greed and hopelessness. We can all be better, do more, offer help. Mr. Abuelo forces us to look and not remain detached and in denial.

Take a deep breath, turn the page, and enter Mr. Abuelo's New York.

Phillip Giambri

Matthew Abuelo

Noises Beyond the Black Snow

Matthew Abuelo

Ode to the Upper West Side

What do you see?
What do you see?
What do you see when you lift the drawn shades?
What kills your reluctance
to perform without
the fear of riding the
express line to common bathrooms
in dead residences.
All of those around you were born
in the season of genius.
Do you understand?

2

Bernie the crier still performs his gimmicks
on his knees
in midtown
as an intrusion to
the beautiful people's senses.
They will forever
only
smile lightly behind drawn shades.
He can turn the tears
on and off
to attract the tourists
for a quick dollar
or the remains of one's dinner.

This game does not work
in the Subways
where everything is allowed
but nothing lasts
and the conductors become ghosts
of the tubes vanishing into the brief points of light
from the A Train.

3

Annie is at it again
walking her dogs for pay
keeping her ear to the concrete
to hear the drum beat of
another developer
whose only love
is to pave over
those who made the scene
and knew how to
play out their part.
She seems so out of place
she feels like a guest in her own skin
waiting for the eviction notice
and the coming
of the true owner of her body
who seems to have been gone
far too long
like the wandering Jew.
Annie still
throws her fortunes to a theater
of incense,
and an audience who lives on their knees
and
whose minds expand
into their
guru's dark room
and burn themselves
into photographs
where the pain
is still
in time
only to drift into the Hudson
riding the tides
beyond the grid
of West 86th Street to
midtown.

4

The chimes promised transcendence
but
those inside
that temple
only found wings
which carried them to
otherwise empty staircases
which do not care for
your coming
or going
up
or
down.
Don't make too much noise
though
because unlike
each stair
your neighbors do not sleep to hide your presence
but slowly grow mad
while living as shut-ins
in their rooms.
This show is not new
it's old.
Here
there are no marquees
or the bright lights of Broadway
only the silent testimonies
of those who sold out
to the brown and tattooed thumb
of the Guru Mai.
But Annie will always surrender to
the hotel that took her beauty
as she smiles after being left behind.
Her face will never dissolve from here
like gray smoke in a rain storm
but it will remain like a finger print in time
which governs where she lives.

5

Karen still is stuck out on the island
where the fury of Ennui
breeds at the cellular level
turning all female minds numb
drained
and used
giving boredom color and weight.
Love here will always turn back on you
like a wild animal that you trusted too long.
In this waste land
all identities and
the pain of being human
break at the property line
and roll back in the waves.

6

Me
I'm in the room
down the hall
where
images and ideas
are stored like newspapers strewn along the floor
and cracked 45s
which kept us all company when
radio died.

This ceiling is designed
for flypaper chandeliers
which secures the last outbreak
of each year
as a farewell to summer.

Each story belongs
to everyone I've stolen from
with a pen or a keyboard.
There is too much stored here to forget
but

my connections have dried up
since we left for Washington Heights
where the real rent
is the payment that the gringo must
pay for his anonymity.
No one here has a name
and the only thing left
is to
pass like a dead jelly fish into the sea.
This room has grown cold
all the radiators bled
and everything saved
frozen in time.
This is preservation
turning all ideas
as pure as photographs taken
on the last ship
to Ellis Island.
Heat
that's where it all breaks down
turning everything you know to ruin.
The only thing I release from these doors
which have formed
two lips under a mustache and beard
are dormant ideas
that gasp to be known
on the sidewalks
at readings
never in universities
where only winter
is the season which meets these words
and sentences
never form
in the frozen air
of politeness.
Do you know this dance?
Never to be sold
there is no money to

be made here.
I'll take the book seller
who sits by the curb
or the hoarder who hasn't been seen for six days.
You can take the clubs
the sweets and the overpriced rooms.
You take the con which comes through in
the waves of ads
and
movies made for those
who only know how to be truly strange
behind drawn shades.

The Body of Good Fortune

The body of good fortune is always fragile
and never lasts.
You understand?
All unseen fortunes gently stroke our synapses
and always turns our direction to Potter's Field
or the penthouse.
The gravity of living in an indifferent city
pulls our hearts to the third rail
so we could feel something
anything but the sensation
perfected by the shut-in.
Insomnia is what remains
like the last roaches
who return long after
the poison has settled under the floorboards.

The Price for Staying Too Long

There is a price for staying too long
in this place
to consume the images of those
who will impose the hell
of needing you
the cruelest of all animals
and
to watch your vanishing
complexities as they disappear
into the rooms of shut-ins.
The hours of isolation
which we hold between our thighs
is plucked from our day
by the friendliest
thieves.
There is no color of being used
only the gray winter of
writer's block.

For a Self-Destructive Heart

What heart have you claimed
by making love in a mad house
where every smile is intent.
Pigment is detail in defining
your ruin.
Here time is a landlord
always on his way with eviction notices
to kick you out of your own body.
But the greater trick is knowing when to leave
or knowing surrender
to permanent winter
that freezes all that is left of our
fortunes
which
fall away into the bathrooms down the hall.
We all hunt for a new source for our failures
which takes the form of rubies
in the pants pocket of saints
who have perfected
the art of throwing themselves
to the embrace of Potter's Field.

It's an easier move
to vanish into our rooms
on the other side of walls
from shut-ins who write themselves out of history
or dance behind drawn shades
under the thumb of wasted hours.
Their minds canceled like dead sharks floating
in the skull,
vacant
with no bite or
direction
and shatter with just one touch.
Their eyes have become fading receptors
which will always take in the images
that flash across the television screen

as imitations of the life four stories
below.
We
You and I
now live in rooms
as vacant as a roach's intent
under the floorboards where there are no stars
only the thunder of expensive shoes.

2

Do you know beauty's final curse
and where it ends
as it fades into another sleepless night
or do you rise above those failures
and waiting rooms
of Cornell
where I sat with lungs
filled with saline bags
impervious to holy air
like jelly fish in the coral sea
only to disappear
with every fleeting hope
of getting out.

3

Escape
is receding into finality's unforgiving ocean.
This is the price we all have to pay
for every time we've realized the futility of charming fate
and making love to our own ruin, our perfected art
which is always waiting for your signature.

Morning's Smoke Detector

The most important noise you will know:
the smoke detector with a dying battery
out in the stairwell
going off every three minutes
with the aggression of bass
coming from passing cars
in Washington Heights
to midtown
and
just loud enough
so
sleep folds in on itself.
Dreaming takes on a different meaning
with a different face

turning from a black and white movie
to yellowed
film
still,
flat
motionless
and all that is left are the waking hours.

It takes technique to escape
the sound that keeps you incarcerated
in an atonal tomb.
Street lights cast
the turning silhouettes
of flypaper in the living room.
And there is always the hope for the hissing of radiators
two months away
when the heat turns moist and heavy
like the collective breath of Argentina.

A Song for No Album at All

The American walked down
the broken lines between east and west
in between is only all the rest
closed down drive-ins,
abandoned factories
and bars with more lonely stories
than customers.
Ed has worked there for 35 years
and heard them all.
From Dale whose wife left him for a used car salesman
from St Louis
and Annie who was raped behind the closed-down mall.

2

From Queens
Manhattan gleams
like ancient Rome.
But in Midtown there is no majesty
it was washed away by the acid rain
and drained down into the Hudson.

3

High above
the stars of Lincoln Center
in their debutante skin
look down on a city which thinks like the future but
moves like an ant hill.
They can afford to keep it on the other side of their door
to watch what comes through that door
with names so delicate
that they die when each letter reaches the air
and falls through the floorboards.
There is something they try to keep clean
by making it
in the shadow of their midtown apartments
like a *femme fatale* in a noir film

with their faces still in the makeup cases.
Behind their eyes, the theater lights go down
over an audience whose demands require
the surrender of a child
and each performance is forgotten
before the applause has died down.
Those doors
act as respite
to those curtains that slowly open
to the sweet terrors
for every performance
under the scent
of make believe's perfume
which reaches the stage
in broken waves
like fingers
pulling every string
to
ruin

4

Down below ghosts move along
the grid looking for their bodies and
names
which were left behind in dive bars
and SROs
that now lay as rubble in
memory.
Their names line rats nests
living off the shores of Ellis Island.
The Hudson churns and releases what you better forget
or be consumed by that memory
They now beg for change with signs that read
"tired and hungry, anything would help."

5

In Jersey the teachers have become enemies of the state
the governor grows fatter from
what the rats left behind.
He says unions are to blame
for bringing the disaster of the Wall Street ship
chained around the throats
of the American as he tries to escape
his time that grows dormant waiting for better days to come.
But there is nothing on the other side of that
dream but another after-hours party of the forgotten
as the lights go down on the city.

(guitar solo plays the song out into a fade.)

Is There Any Hell Worse Than Now

Is there any hell greater than now?
We have become shut-ins in our own craniums
where clenched jaws become drawn shades.
Did you know that we've reached the end?
This program curdles
and disintegrates like old film
which touches the air for the first time in 50 years.

The roaches under the floorboards take the forms of
those television hours spent
in the dry winter of insomnia
like useless subway tokens
passed off to the cats who beg for change along 14th street
as dimes or pennies.

What savior do you still search for in these silent stations?
Don't you know they all left a long time ago
hanging themselves in their closets
in their rooms on 86 street
or living like ghosts when
the weight of drunken dances
of those who know only need
becomes a new gravity
turning coal to diamonds.

Never stay too long
here
in the room of your waking hours.
Every space becomes a prison
after a while
and every prison
becomes a padded room
for those who have surrendered.

The wealthy walk pretty
in their perfect skin.
Black girls

look at each other with distrust on the A train
with knife fights in their eyes.
Theirs are tiny wars older
than the Robert Moses landscapes
or the blue flame which acts as the soft chain
of addiction.

When the tongue becomes numb and stifled
or forgotten
then it is clear that we have to leave.
Where the hell is our New York anyway?
And when our words bend under the weight of a family's demands
or suffocated by the tyranny of their love
then their love will be realized in the
method of perfection
in your ruin.

If I decide to leave my head
then I will realize that all my friends
are so much older.
Serving as a reminder of the future
their stories told with broken
or incomplete frames
of fragile film.
Will I be toothless
or walk around in moth-eaten jackets,
screaming about politics
and will these thirty somethings still want to fuck me?

Give me the burning landfill of this past
giving off black plums of smoke and the smell of tar.
The past smells of tar when it burns
don't ask me why
but it can be seen
from the far window inside the Cloisters
next to a French man's tapestry.
When will it burn out?

When will I learn not to burn out
to avoid newspaper pasts
where all stories run together
with the first strong rain of the year
as ink?
All that is left are the museums of what
disappears with the lightening.

The Gun Is Loaded

Why do I still make love to the city which sits
on the other side of my window
waiting for the final eviction notice from its place in time
and forgotten in Potter's Field
nameless on the cutting room floor
in an advertising office somewhere in midtown?
We sit Shiva under the street lights
bright as a moon.
There are no prayers here
for subway divers
delaying the 6 line for several hours.
Those long distance meditations
have come at too high of a price
and are no replacements for the telephone.
They only deaden the sensation
of being flushed out of your apartment
and lay in waste
in the meaningless arcade
of exiled futures
that are not futures
but blank canvas
and
stripped of our names
and language
and has been recalled
or relegated to life under the floorboards
where all thunder comes from high heel shoes.

2

Do you know the supernova that has consumed the city's voice
or the resentment of what's left behind
born of the Clorox tide designed to wipe the city clean
of all memories of those who flung themselves out of their windows
to taste the pavement if only for one last moment
the source of their torment?
With the right tongue

you can still sense them in each leaf of grass
which covers the landfill of memory.
The essence never really recedes.
It is the ghost of ruin
and the price of beauty
that the body must pay in full.
Even in suicide time
on some strange night
during a rare blackout in the city
you can go into any of those (SRO) rooms
and still feel the moment when the rope tightened
and the neck snapped
and silence flowered
and the great escape achieved.

Defying Death While at the Movies

Our futures now
lie in the movies
for all younger generations
content falls into the gloss of advertisements
before each show.
The cutting room floor is where our time grows shorter
and pushes us closer
to being nameless in Potters Field.
That's why I dig Kurosawa films
where in three and a half hours
we are all immortal.

For Mr. Algren

Why do we race for the scrap heaps of all forgotten things?
Is it to watch the plumes of smoke
bellowing from a future
which is not a future but wasted hours waiting
for men and women to finally stand
but who
never stood for anything at all?
Do you understand?
And what are the solutions
when the young become as brutal as New York City landlords
turning our buildings into hotels
for out of towners who walk pretty
in their cocksure skin
with its perfect glow
and whose gravity broadens the shoulders of
those who live with bent backs
for the labor of becoming exhibits
or plunge into the world
of the mole people.
As one mayor put it
"New York is open for business."
The brutality Mr. Algren is that only the truly wealthy
can own a judge
and getting off on a misdemeanor is afforded only to
those who can pay the price of admission for staying out of the Tombs
It is the unspoken law born from the advertisement rooms
that convinces the broker
and the bartender
that this is the natural order of things.

2
Are we the new Indians
to be buried under the ruins
that were our rooms
or the bathroom that sat at the end of the hall?

Oh New York

On New York
with your buildings as clean as ancient Rome
would you have the waters of the Hudson River
wash us away into the oceans
and our breath bleached from your air?
And what are air rights other than
a rich man's attempt to claim the horizon as his own?
Are we to wash up on the shores of Plum Island
with all the newspapers
used syringes and Coney Island whitefish?
Even the taxi driver who passes through the nights
on streets that are nowhere avenues to him
will never call the great pinball machine of Time Square
home.
His place is across the George Washington Bridge
where he disappears
into the view across the Hudson.
Someone saw to that a long time ago
in some backroom deal.

You can't love a city
unless you love its ghosts
who will always haunt the SRO of the heart.
They are all there:
the subway suicide diver,
whose last act of desperation delayed the 1 train for 6 hours.
The squeegee man
who will forever clean passing windshields
at new intersections
with old
and
soiled water,
The shut-in
who lost her mind only to be locked up in Saint Luke's.
The street artist who found his lot among other street artists in
Washington Square Park
before freezing to death in the embrace of winter.

And all of the iron workers
whose words will never make it into the history books
as dirty faced testimonies of those buried under the concrete
of a story white washed.
Richard who wound up on the streets
after being evicted
from the apartment he was born in
for being a hoarder
only to be let back in a few months later
then dying in the hospital two weeks after.
There is the cop who was shot in the head up in the Bronx
And the punk still looking for a place to play
now that CBGB is gone.
I've seen these ghosts vanish in the exhaust
from passing taxi cabs
only to be shit out behind
all metal doors.
Sometimes I feel that they found a natural home
in my skull where they form abscesses
on my
brain
making it impossible to meditate on any emergency
which amplifies all my anxieties
that now are breaking through the wall of Prozac.

A question to the city from a letter

"Are you really a dying arcade?"

Paris 1918

I see Paris 1918 in the steam of manhole covers
down on Columbus Circle
when the music was sweeter to the ear
and the smell of art
didn't emanate from the advertising
firms with their resentments
of those who surrender to
the clinics.
Do you know this idiot romance
for a storied time I could never ask to be in
nor navigate its gravity if I was.
But I'd like to step out
before I become just another
nameless asshole
in a waltz to Potter's Field.

Did it come too early
or
did I come too late?
After all
the bathrooms of cheap hotels sat empty
then
without meaning?
Today they wait for the winter of crime
in its frozen embrace
born of a landlord's wet dream
of turning his building
into just another museum
of those who knew the city's polluted breath
which still reeks of
a felony born of
all the final deals which were signed
and delivered
behind the closed doors of board rooms.

Anxieties had a different color then.
Not black like the late December snow
of New York
but the dead white prick of an opium dream.
Will I still long for this escape when the alcohol is all gone?
And should I escape the clinic
where yellowed suicide letters
litter the floors?
If not
what else should we toast to?

Management
(From *Before Snow Turns Black*)

They were of the feral kind.
No common con-men,
highway men
or small time crooks
or any self respecting junkies
would have anything to do with them,
much less trust 'em.
They were bred by the landlords for
the lone purpose of clearing out the
buildings.
There were no depths of depravity that they wouldn't crawl.
Those whose floorboards split in two
could look down and see the eyes of this staff
looking back up at them,
in roach-skin suits.
The only thing colder than their black loveless eyes
was the endless winter in their hearts
where all humanity was frozen in time like an extinct species
and their souls would forever serve sentences in unknown prisons of their
own making.

Land of the Cheated

It occurred to Sam that all the clocks on all the business walls no longer kept track of the minutes or even the hours of each day. Instead, they measured the drudgery of the grocery cashier and the convenience store clerk alike. What ticked away on these clocks was no longer time but the overtime hours robbed from each worker by each manager. But despite their position, both clerk and boss knew that they would forever live on shut-in hours, where all fantasies were teenage dreams of something better and had replaced the reality that years no longer mattered in the land of the cheated; one always flowed into another and they all seemed the same somehow. Even those who lived in the moments of being stoned on weed or pills could escape this plane for so long, but would always come crashing down, back to this yearless land. Those who knew how to navigate through these waters like so many fish in a clear glass bowl always moved with the instinct to survive but with no will to live. The embrace of Prozac took care of that long ago.

New York's Bad Dream

New York used to be a squatters town
and
a misfits town
and a union town.
This is where you could
find a cheap room at the Chelsea
or the Dexter House
with a bathroom down the hall.
Or at the Commander.
Many SROs vanished into the
remains of burnt out
warehouses once run by
"who wants to know industries"
only to succumb to the midnight storms
of "Jewish lightning."
This was the town
where the truly strange
and burned out radicals sat at diners with
coffee stained napkins
sitting under coffee stained cups
screaming about the price of rent
or the loss of tenements under the weight of Lincoln Center.
Here punks
Rabbis
the smiling hustler
and the honest con men
and the artist
were the Lower East Side
and where one could always find a cheap meal
of well-cooked dumplings
across from CBGB
or at the Wo Hop in China Town
where the cops and locals gathered
but where out-of-towners passed without notice.

Our liberal mayor Koch
declared that it was official policy

that City Hall would no longer worry about
the poor or the homeless
and forced them to the outer boroughs
with one stroke of a pen.
And when more cardboard communities
sprung up like cattails in a polluted heart
than bodies removed from Manhattan
or placed in Potter's Field
the gun was handed over
to a whiney crossdressing ex-prosecutor
who was placed in the Mayor's chair
turning the homeless into outlaws under the lights of Broadway
and the theaters were vacated
for the price of the SRO heartbeat.
City Hall unleased the Clorox tide, at last
washing away the pimps
the artists
the squeegee men
the graffiti
the honest panhandler
and the grinning hustler
and the avenue corner whores
while keeping those on the Wall Street payroll
in place
even New York was washed clean
of a genius that grew through
all the cracks
and warehoused apartments
and all the wards
and the discos
like cat-tails
in a polluted heart.
For those who
never saw morning
or for those whose morning came too soon
subway diving onto the third rail
under the graffiti walls
of midtown became just another pastime.

You could always tell what borough you were in
by the local baseball fans.
The Mets would find no home in the Bronx
while the Yankees received the Bronx cheer in Queens.
In Brooklyn
the Dodgers will be forever hated
or dead.
The last ticket has been punched at Ebbets Field.
This is the great indignity that came by way of
learning the true game of sports
and is passed down as a birthright
for all native Brooklynites
even those not yet born.
This indignity of a team moving from the borough
of loyal saints
to the city for fair-weather angels
which sits as a scar on the soul
of everyone who must now look up
just to find love in Potter's Field.

While Manhattan has no face for any of the teams
unless it's the playoffs.

It is still a town of Dutch oven summers
where the concrete is hotter than the 85 degree air.
The heat keeps everyone in the subways on edge
with the fear of an undefined but always present threat.

Now this where the truly cheated outrun their debts
only to be taken by another deal
from those who make a living
through 1964 World's Fair promises
of a clean future only afforded
to those whose wallets are as thick as the
Sunday edition of the New York Times
while all others dream of escaping
the old processing plant
of the Tombs

which delivers another gone tenant
to another landlord
like room service
churning out the nameless assholes
to the yearless avenues.

The only con greater than the subway sermons
are the real estate deals
which turn judges
into executioners
tenants into the condemned
and the landlords into judges.

This has become the town
where events
and
places are named after artists
who could not afford to live there
were they still alive.
There is Ginsberg's Howl Festival
Café Mozart
and Poe's restaurant.

This has never been a town
of permanence.
Each bar
each diner and each building
vanish as quick as the subway conductor's face
into the forward tunnel
and faster than a breath
but with the sound of passing thunder.
Nothing is ever left behind.
Not the memory of what was where
or the names of those swept
out to the suburbs
or even those
who
fell out of time and onto
the subway platforms.

This city has never been a morning town.
New York has always been an insomniac's town.
All of its true professionals
its night workers
have become nothing more
than just another commodity
for the wealthy squares who vanish on the other side
of the George Washington Bridge
or across the L.I.E
or
the exit to White Plains.

And from across the midtown tunnel
from the Long Island of the cheated
the bored children of the Exodus
have escaped their garrisons known as villages
and have decided to return
to the city
as if coming back
to a holy land.
The only price is their souls
which become tainted meat
for landlords
to lay their gospel of the rented truth
of the tenements.

2

What is the labor pool
but a discount bin which is rummaged through by only
the truly wealthiest fingers
looking to cheat the hopelessly cheated?

Stonewall blew up
in the face of the NYPD
where night sticks were replaced
by high heeled shoes
that came down on the skulls
of bloodthirsty cops
like the Congo rain.

Traffic,
that is the only consistency
in the cheated heart of an indifferent city.

Here in each
of these rooms
dirt and steam heat are neither friend
nor enemy
but the last things we can trust
until the next rent demand
or visit to housing court.
And all good fortune ends
when you are reduced to walking through
the street light and neon store front parade
like a moth through a flame
with no thought of coming out alive.

The power brokers
the Wall Street boys
the real estate boards
the college boards of NYU
and Columbia
and advertisement boards
are the true gods of New York
basking with their inflated egos
made of junk bonds
but sooner or later they all
get dragged down to the street level
and torn apart like so many toys
which outstayed their welcome
when the payoff becomes too great a price
or when they are recalled when the sales run dry.
But Catholic guilt
and Albany
will reflate these holy egos
while "Jewish lightning" burns down
the tenements and SROs built before the gods were born.
This is the season of crime.

3

This is the town where all its squatters
knew the good deal of the warehoused apartment building
and the art of tapping the city's power lines.
Where rents meant nothing
and communities began to flower
in the squatter's victory garden
while those in Saint Luke's saw their fortunes run dry.
Sooner or later all the state's
and the country's radicals
found themselves pressed against
the gilded walls of Madison Ave.
And whose fists splintered the closed doors
of Park Avenue
where the true crimes take place
where the truly wealthy rig the game
for all Wall Street players
on the back of the longshoreman
long ago.

This is the town under the wary gaze from the eyes
of the suburbs from those
who always wait for the last squatter
to die in the silent room of the wards
or the unfeeling streets.
This is where the punk rockers
flowered along the Bowery
like ragweed
in the furious winds of two minute songs.
They were the last of those whose souls would never be for sale
only to be worn out on the black snow sidewalks
and along the tattooed walls.
But the tide of the No Wave
washed over the lower east side
as Lydia Lunch's loaded gun pointed at every
square heart ripe to be crushed under the weight of true poetry.

This was the town of accents
from all the old countries.

The bending of each word
by each speaker
was as if they were marked
by the touch of those boroughs
which they called a natural home.

Each block was a country
each neighborhood was a nation.
With the poetry of their accents
locals without pretention
took a number at the local delis
in the hope of scoring their corned-beef
or Pumpernickel bread.
Now they will forever be waiting in lines
with numbers that will never be called.
Their countries and nations are now gone
having been washed away by the great flood
of the west.

To find those accents in the year of our lord
2015
you have to go deep into the archives of any library
or read from the stenographer's
reports taken down
in cases
overseen by judges for hire
owned by the truly wealthy
with the funds to white-out
American letters of discontent
in a system where the game is rigged
and the only marker for the forgotten
is a coffin with a serial number.

What we have all learned
Heaven is the tenement with no landlords at all.

For it is the landlords and building owners alike
who have turned the firehoses
on the artists born in the season of genius

and whose words and paintings
and films were as gray as the streets that they adorned
as being beautiful in its crude language
and dangerous reproach.
For it was the language
of those who looked up
not for another past time
but to the idea that the stars were
the big stage for all those children who once wore safety pins
and cable wire just to keep their pants up.
The chance of being on TV was just around the corner.

These were the writers who wrote themselves out of favor
with academia and onto the yellowed pages of forgotten books
which now collect dust in a warehouse.
While its musicians could close their eyes and listen to the sound
of the incoming one train
or the heavy traffic on the Henry Hudson
and hear the beat and the rhythm
of each note
of each beat
of the city's heart.
Some finally made it big
and now live above the streets or in some other town.
Ok Miss Midler we remember you when you were still singing in
bathhouses
while squares were being blown
by transsexuals too low to call the cops
or to get a taxi home.
Did you ever say
that peasants are among my ranks
and
I'm among theirs
Or did you sing on indifferently?

Today New York City acts as a wino in the last throes
of alcohol sickness.
Having replaced itself
with a glossed dream of mediocrity.

You can see this dream in all the lifestyle magazines
which have replaced art
with banality and boredom
of bad artists.
The city would lose itself altogether
were it not for the stains on its clothes
of an excess it would sooner forget.
Its new skin
is that of a museum city
where you can find the past
it still tries to live off of
and which out-of-towners embrace
because of all the "cool books"
and movies
just as long as it never again
leaves its display case where everything is safe.
Even the Chelsea now has been wiped clean
of all art
and is now open to gray suit business men
and gawking European tourists.

Like any other museum city,

London
Paris
and
Chicago

New York leans heavily on its main attractions
some borne from 9/11
others which once belonged
to the wild eyed natives.
Ground zero was the great hole in the
ground for all gawkers
from all the corners of the earth
to come and stare slack jawed.
That hole has only grown though,
swallowing one community after another
and in their place new featureless buildings

as weeds in a once proud garden.
9/11 turned into the greatest land grab by the world's wealthy
since the Trail of Tears.

The once great port city of misfits
Weirdos
Outcasts
and the truly brilliant
is now gone for good
having found an eviction notice on its door.

4

The great cliché of New York
"When this city sneezes the world gets a head cold."
The virus is the Robber Baron class.
There is nowhere left in New York law
or culture where their presence isn't felt.
Along the northern wall of Lincoln center and on a banner on the front
of the museum of natural history
David and Charles Koch's names
become the main attraction.
And what about the Rockefellers?
They are still the most hated family
by the old timers here.
They walked through the streets
throwing pennies to the peasants
when everything cost a dime
and until recently
a kid caught with weed
could get the same sentence as a murderer.
Their reach, both the Koch's
and the Rockefellers alike,
is far beyond the political world
of this city and reaches for the throats
of anyone who can't pay the rent.

The Brief Story of Henry Wilson

Henry Wilson looked out the only window of his single room and onto the street below. The iron colored light of late winter made everything outside look gray somehow. The swirling snow and wind created eddies along the sidewalk as passersby moved like so many fish is a bowl, hunched over with their faces pointed to the ground. Mothers with their kamikaze strollers were used to move along any straggler who moved too slowly for any wealthy mother to afford. He had been among the ranks of those out there, long ago but was now living as a shut-in, only leaving his apartment to go grocery shopping or go to the bank or to pick up his mail which included his monthly welfare check. His parents had, when he was still a boy, their Victory garden which by this time had long wilted along with last vapors of the American dream. In a strange way, which Henry could never fully explain, he felt that these checks were payment for his family's services to the country during the Second World War. His father was a war resister while his mother worked as a nurse state side taking care of the institutionalized and destroyed by "battle fatigue."

After the war overseas, the war at home started, Senator Joseph McCarthy sent out his goon squads to hunt down accused Communists from every walk of life, every ally way, every street corner and every movie studio. Without explanation his parents wound up on the list as did their neighbors who lived across the hall of a three story walk up in the East Village. Like so many others, they were forced underground, many moving into basements out on the Island or into the deserts of Mexico and wilderness of Canada. For the truly hunted who were forced too far below the waterline of polite society, they forgot about the idea of believing in God while many came to consider preachers, priests and rabbis as con men of the highest orders and snake oil salesmen of the lowest class. Still others who hit the times' bedrock, figured that they were too far below ground that even if there was a God, he must have surely forgotten about them. After all, no angel could fly to such depths, that they would not get lost. The Jews among their ranks soon realized that the heavens were long empty and the sky was forever indifferent to any prayer or scorn. For the soot that bellowed from the smokestacks of Auschwitz still blanketed their memories and buried any need for a Torah whose words now lay hollow.

The pressure of being hunted became too much for his father to bare. Wilson watched his old man spiral into the throes of paranoia and alcohol's cruelest ocean. Even after McCarthy had his great melt down on national

TV, the old man swore there was an FBI agent around every corner. Pretty soon, he was convinced that the radio was a kind of transmitter which allowed authorities to keep track of the family at all times. These fits led Wilson's father to spend time in and out of psych wards until he was found hanging with a piece of cable wire around his throat in the laundry room of their apartment building. But that was all long ago.

The fear that was born from those days had hunted Henry down and sentenced him to a life among piles of clothing, movie cases and yellowed newspapers. And every day he promised himself he would leave his apartment and join the world of the living. But this promise was always going to take place tomorrow until all his plans were pushed to all the tomorrows which he would ever know. The anxieties had become just too great and the paralysis caused by such fear had long reduced him to a house cat, forever looking out the window at a world he knew he would never be a part of again. The time spent between the four walls may have kept his body in a womb of dry wall and bricks but the steady sound of the clocks on his walls, along with the endless glare of his television set, sent his mind drifting into the yearless avenues where time long dissolved and where there were no police officers unravelling their flypaper to catch the never ending stream of the accused only to dump them into the tombs. He, Henry Wilson, alone escaped the barricades. For he had discovered the SRO of the heart and that room had just gotten larger and all of a sudden believed himself to be the saint of the cheated soul. But he was no agent of God but of man. For how could he serve any God who was noticeably absent when he and his family entered the bedrock of the Bellevue wards? Wilson swore the ghost of his father was still there strapped down to the same bed, heavily drugged and barely able to utter a comprehensive sentence. There were many a time that the old man was passed out and all his mother could do was hold his hand and weep softly as not to disturb another patient who also resided in the antiseptic room. From somewhere down the hall, the smell of piss and shit hung heavy in the ward's air and all the visitors did their best not to succumb to the stench which greeted them like an overly friendly security guard.

Now it was a matter of finding the evidence of his holiness and a place to lead his flock. "Only if I had a sign" Henry stated out loud to no one. Images started rolling along his eyelids of him leading great masses into the either where rent means nothing because there are no landlords in his new city of the condemned. "I'd rather be a loser with endless dreams than America's hero with no dreams left at all. I am of the pauper's ranks and they are of mine and I would rather have a serial number on my coffin then some stupid headstone."

Loud moaning came from the other side of the wall nearest to his bed. It was Apu, an Indian Englishman with an outbreak of shingles which had spread across his back and chest. There was no position he could lay for very long before turning back and forth with clenched teeth. His desperate moaning had gone on for well over ten days and seemed to have little chance of being cured. His Hindu upbringing kept him away from western medicine, and turned instead to Ayurvedic therapy. He had long thrown his lot behind one of New York City's guru of Siddha Yoga, where the wealthy and the cheated alike came to gather in chants of transcendence. The guru lead each and every ceremony, looking at her followers as a feast of fools, all of whom owned a copy of the DVDs she produced with this or that lecture on surrendering the self to God as the universe. But anyone who would have looked in on these gatherings would have wondered if she had surrendered herself to anything at all. Now there was little he could do but surrender himself to the pain of each small attack on his nerve endings which felt like they were opening like flowers under the bellowing light of every unforgiving day. In a strange sense, this illness became Apu's awakening into something holy, his one chance to surrender to the endless alleyways of humility. It is what happens to anyone whoever followed a con artist that came to believe her own con. Somewhere in her robes and veils her body still twitched with the anticipation of one businessman looking to screw another.

Now on his sweat soaked mattress, under the scented air of incense, Apu faced the most unforgiving light of all, the one that left no corner of the con he set for himself unexposed, giving him the feeling of a detective who was investigating a murder which he knew he committed. It was a con that ran deeper than any scar of the soul. For the first time he started begging out loud for someone to call for an ambulance. "Poor bastard" Wilson lamented with a distant voice. "He must be one of my flock."

A loud banging came from his door. Wilson didn't need to ask who it was, a voice with a thick polish accent came from the hall, "You fuckin' welfare tenants need to pay more money. How dare you live here so much on the cheap. The boss will get you out, you will see. We will get good people in here." It was the super of the building, Boris, who also took the role of one of the landlord's goons along with being a useful idiot and drunken buffoon who danced for every scrap off the landlord's table. To Wilson, the voice from the other side of the door could just as easily been an FBI agent's, finally triggering the trap which they've been setting for more than 50 years now. But it was the other voices in the halls, the ones that had become far too familiar which scared Wilson the most. They always seemed to have the vague urgency of the sirens of passing emergency vehicles, racing down West End Avenue. "Shut the fuck up you gypsy piece of shit!" another voice shouted back.

"I'm Polish not Romanian. You see? You ignorant people don't know nuthin'."

"I don't care you're still a cheap gypsy fuck to me!"

Wilson could hear the Pole's heavy boots stomp across the section floor before he opened the security door, letting it slam just behind him.

Wilson continued to look out the window onto the street as the snow fell at an angle. A homeless man passed under the last reminiscence of daylight, pushing a shopping cart filled with soda cans. He moved quickly towards Broadway. The section door opened again, this time closing with no sound. Light footsteps moved across the hallway and into the community bathroom. Cries rang throughout the section.

"Those Jews, they run everything. They don't care. Those pigs. They don't care I'm sick. Those fuckin' Jews make it hard for me to get my AIDs medicine. They no care, no one cares for poor Julio. What they care? They have all the money! No one cares if I live or die. Poooor Julio. Poooor Julioooo!"

Then the bathroom door closed and all Wilson could hear were heavy sobs from Julio who was desperately trying to hold on to the last vestiges of his sanity. The constant intake of drug cocktails which kept him alive was robbing him of his connection to the world and led him to sounding off in long rants down in the subway stations till the police would cart him off to the wards of Bellevue. Henry turned to his door. "Why does he go on like that and who are all these Hebrews in his head who keep conspiring against him? Where is his father among them? The old man was a rabbi. Was his mother's tongue really that much of a Catholic shot gun? Did she really splatter the old man's name all over the wall in that poor bastard's mind?" Wilson's eyes dropped to the floor in time to see a large bull roach scurry behind a book case without any noise.

On the side of a building across the street, Wilson saw a concentrated light, not unlike the glare of a TV set in the morning light. Henry cried out, "This is my sign. My guiding star to deliver the great flock back to the God that has long forgotten about each and every one of them!" Without a second thought Henry Wilson opened his window in order to go to that light. He crawled out with great urgency, falling four stories down. Long sharp spikes from the gate below shot through his eye sockets, snapping his neck. His shins and knee bones shattered against the concrete of the sidewalk which sent a sudden current of pain up his spine and created a thunderous roar in his skull. Blood ran slowly from his eye sockets down the long black metal of the fence forming small red pools in the snow that began to form rivers flowing towards the gutters. The last thought raced through his mind, "I'm the true saint of the people. All will be delivered home". For the first time in days the snow had finally stopped falling as the crowd gathered to stare at the idol on the metal fence, who died for no one's sins at all. But the wind was colder and bitterer as if it was just another heart with a grudge in a city full of grievances. From all the nearby stores and all the nearby bars, Christmas music echoed through the streets. Fathers passed by with their families, looking only for a moment at the commotion on the sidewalk, with mild annoyance while cab drivers rubbernecked the bridge and tunnel crowd to get a look at the action. And all the unseen ghosts sang their unheard carols, "Henry Wilson chose a casket marked with a serial number in a grave with no head stone, not a name nor a home. He escaped the winter when the season had become so swollen, before his mad soul could be stolen. He finally delivered his flock of the fallen. Henry Wilson the saint of the SRO."

Nine stories up a young child took a pocket mirror out of the fading sun where he was bending the light and creating a dim glare on the building across the street. Wilson's guiding star vanished as the child stuck the mirror in his dresser drawer. He was called to the dining room table indifferent to the action below to eat with his indifferent family.

Last Love Letter

Oh to vacation behind the heavy metal door
to escape another election year.
All news is stopped at the door by the guards
who
forever sit in the same place.
Waiting
always
waiting to retrieve all banned goods
and outside time.
Between med time
and bed time is empty time
where those evicted from their bodies
are stuck staring at their feet.
But all have the midnight carousal
under their tongues
"If that bitch doesn't give me my meds
I'm going to kick that door down.
Either that door will break or my leg will."

The one mercy in the sexless hotel
memories fall way.
Memories of what building was torn down.
What now empty store front housed
the latest failure
now lays in the darkened reminder of memory
and acts as a constant reminder of becoming what is left behind
in this
the city of
of the buried
and forgotten.
In their place every mind
is fixed
with a retread with no memories at all.

But retreads always fall off and litter the roads
before we re-enter to antiseptic air.
Only letters are allowed past the guards
I can't remember the last time we received a letter.
Its all emails
and telephone calls these days.
Perhaps this is how I lost my sense
of anticipation.
When was the last time
I sent a letter?
Inside
we all can sleep the sleep of the forgotten.
Some of us have gotten our fill of the stars
and prefer a ceiling to an indifferent sky
and empty heavens.
All others from these ranks who never returned
have wandered beyond
the light of day
into the trainless subway tunnels
and into the fold
of the disconnected brotherhood/sisterhood
of the mole people.

The Mole People

This is the real lost tribe of America
living beyond the reach of landlords
and their thugs for hire.

For each there is no need to peer into the shadows
of yet another condo.
Their hidden jungle
is not of the Amazon
but the Subway system
where no natural light ever penetrates.
The soul is the first
and cheapest thing
to leave behind.
I've heard the tribe will let you in
as long as you mind
Your own business.
The one felony never to commit
is to look for someone
any one
to tell about something
that has haunted you your
whole life.
It is best to be a nameless asshole
among the ranks of other nameless assholes.
There are no eviction notices at these depths.
Yet.
Their moon comes
with the thunder overhead
from passing cars.

Those who wish to be forgotten,
stay forgotten
and are certain to replace
the hopes for a headstone with that of a serial number
marked for a pauper's grave.

Matthew Abuelo

This is the wish of the shut-in
to die nameless in their SROs
or over priced
one bedroom pad
in Washington Heights.
(Hiding from who?)
Hiding from those they wish to forget.
A psychotic lover
whose love is serrated
and cuts too deep
till it reaches bone.
Their own home town
which they attempted to cut the tether to
in a desperate escape.
Or death.
Death is what comes too cheap for most
and too soon for some
or too late for all others.
But if you dance forever you will never die.

The Clocks

Here clocks talk to each other
of all the collected hours
by those who live by the clock
or all who can exist in confined rooms
as a natural environment
with a waiting bathroom down the hall
and one foot on the third rail.
The shut-in turns a blind eye to the amateurs
who fear being forgotten
several stories down.

2
After all the deals are made
and all the SROs torn down
and those of us who grow tired of waiting for the eviction
notices to be handed down by a judge on the take
have moved on
or held our ground
and after all New York
becomes "open for business"
every street becomes just another bazaar,
and when those who have been out to sea for far too long
and wish to return home
are met by closed port cities
with indifferent silence
Even the circus of your life has moved on
long ago.
Do you care?
The noise of the carousels have become muted.

You can peer closely through the crowds
to see the better ghosts
among us
the last of the American Tribe
forever flailing in the
last light of late evening
fading.

Untitled

I'd prefer to spend time with those who
know the art of losing well
with bitterness in their heart
than the man who exists with indifference.
The natural loser has perfected his art
and means it.
Behind his jaw the gun is always loaded
and the third rail forever lies beneath his tongue.
Do not underestimate the accuracy of each word
or the distance of his fire.

The man who walks with indifference
shows the same lack of discipline usually
afforded to an only child
and he has no meaning at all.

Untitled

I owe too much to those I've stolen from.
I'm a thief of stories
didn't you know that?
And more importantly
do you care?
I've watched each one (story)
wilt into the dead soul
of comedy.
You need to handle them as fine china
and with a master's green thumb
designed
to make an ascending wilderness grow.
Holding back each story
is not unlike keeping a sharp stone
under your tongue.
Sure you can do it
for awhile
but sooner or later
your mouth will bleed.
Not with blood
but with words
which flow like heavy traffic on 11th Ave.
just before rush hour.

Two Simple Facts

Among the wagers
and the lust for blood
no one listens to the ceiling fan
over the title fight.

2
All the dying children
of the holy and rotting corpse
have made it a habit of crawling to the glowing light
to
find
nothing
at all.
The greatest joke played on mankind.

A Random Thought

The nameless roll by with dirty faces
looking for money to fold
and have replaced their head stones with serial numbers
while their comrades in arms
sleep the sleep
of the forgotten
in moving subway cars.
They exude the yellow smell
of the truly sick.
God is never afforded to those who reach this floor.
I watch this show
as a future which is too near
and always calling.
Yet the pigeons seem fine
never having to stake their claim,
their bands have an eternal understanding.
But the sea gulls continue to beg
for whatever it is
you're eating at the time
while
Coney Island whitefish continue to float by
unnoticed.
All the roaches find a natural home
in all the SRO's
and the kitchens
in the Chinese restaurants.
And all the beautiful people
will continue to walk by with
newly fashioned indifference.
No Mr. Bowles
the cage door is not always open.
It is
in fact
always locked
and the net always tightens
for those who are not afforded the key.

What door is open to
the men and
women
who sit on the sidewalks with signs that read
"Tired and hungry. Even change will help,"
and sleep in the nights of neon digital lights
which glow purple some of the time
but colorless most of the time.
But the pigeons will always be fine.

Goodbye Sergeant

It was the first day of spring and the season for the Tombs to send convicted prisoners upstate to serve their prison sentences had just begun. The bus had just arrived to pick up the men who were now being warehoused for pickup. Sergeant William Horowitz walked down the room of the holding cells, followed by two larger policemen, one with a shotgun held tightly against his breast. Inside the first cell was a tall black kid, who was no older than eighteen, wearing his blue jeans just high enough to cover his crotch, and a white sleeveless tee-shirt. The kid had a long jagged scar on one cheek from what William could only assume was from a fight or being jumped by fellow kids from his neighborhood.

"Ok son, grab the bars, your ride is here." William remarked with a bored tone in his voice.

This job had become so routine, he knew what response to expect from each prisoner based on the look in their eyes. The kid straightened up to display his full height in an empty attempt to intimidate his jailers. The kid's face was hardened but his eyes showed the same fear as those animals who know their end was around the corner or down some long corridor.

"You white mother fuckers sold my black ass to them upstate hicks! No black man gets a break in this country for nuthin. Congratulations cop, you got your prize nigga. Things never fuckin' change."

"Yes it's all the white man's fault you're here. Had nothing to do with that cannon you blasted into the clerk's chest at the bodega I suppose."

"I didn't shoot no fuckin clerk, your boys grabbed the first nigga they could find to set up for this bullshit. What you need a suspect, your boys come to the Bronx and grab the first brother they could find? That damn judge and everyone in the court room knows I didn't have nuthin to do with that clerk getting shot."

"Well you're the winner of the lottery then, grab the bars."

"Man, I got set up I'm telling you! I'm innocent, man. Listen to me!"

"Is that why they found your finger prints on the gun left at the scene? Look Reggie, we're just holding you here. The judge set the sentence and he is God in that court room. Now hurry up I don't have all day."

Before the kid could protest further, the cop with the shotgun cocked the barrel. The argument had suddenly ended. The kid grabbed the bars as William opened the jail doors and the guards entered shackling the prisoner's wrists and ankles. He was frog walked a few feet out of the cage, then was taken by another guard to a hall way just outside the room.

William walked two cells down where he was greeted by an old and heavily tattooed biker with long white hair which rested on a leather vest which was a size too small for the biker's frame. His back was pressed against the far wall of the cell with one booted foot supporting him the other leg was bent and his foot rested on the wall. He was thin and strangely pale with a yellow tint. The skin of his face was stretched tight over his sharp cheek bones giving him the look of an old Indian.

"Back again Sal? What are you in for now?"

"Had a talk with some little shit bartender. You know the kind. Some little twenty something shithead ain't goin to talk to nobody no more."

"You mean you beat the kid to death while on crystal meth? What was the argument about there?"

"I told him to turn up the volume on the tv behind the bar, baseball game was on and I told that mother I had fifty bucks on the game. That little piece of shit acted as if he didn't hear me. I know he heard me when I pulled his ass across the bar before I beat the shit out of him with my bar stool."

"Well Sal you're going to have plenty of time to watch the game where you're going. You know the routine. Let's get on with it."

The biker walked to the front of the cell and grabbed the bars and once again William opened the jail door and the two guards shackled the prisoner's wrists and ankles. Two other guards came in and marched him down the hall.

William moved on to the next cell. In the cage was a tranny-professional woman in a miniskirt with high heel shoes. Her long blond hair fell loosely on her shoulders while strands were caught up in the caked makeup which, along with a five o'clock shadow and deep lines in her face gave her the look of old New York with its hopeless avenues which provided such women with a career.

"Says here you're here for offing a John."

"No I would never do that, I'm a professional girl. I treat all my customers well. I'm a woman who gives these men something extra if you know what I mean. You believe me, don't you?"

"Why did they find you with the guy's wallet?"

"Oh I found it on the ground. I wanted to make sure he got it back. I was going to mail it back to him."

"What? An empty wallet"?

"What people do with their stuff is none of my business."

"Why did they find the John's body with a switch blade in his jugular, seven blocks from where you were picked up?"

"Was he? Oh that's terrible, I would never do such a thing. Never!"

"Well the jury sent your sweet ass upstate. Besides I have no say about it. Says here you were in Bellevue. What were you in for?"

"My rooommate called 911 telling them I was tryin' to kill myself. Can you imagine? She said I was slashing my wrists. That's so crazy."

"Is that the reason for the marks on your arms?"

"No that was from some fuckin' john who got too rough."

"I think you've cracked a long time ago but that's for the doctor's upstate to decide."

He sighed deeply then moved onto the next cell. In the fourth and final cell sat to be emptied, sat a painfully thin Honduran whose face was in his hands, weeping deeply.

"Christ, Juan, you're in here again? What? You like this place so much? What are you in for this time?"

The man looked up with tears still streaming from his eyes. He attempted a toothless smile but the gesture only made him look more broken down.

"I beat my wife, I was drunk and so mad."

"Well you'll have all the time you need to dry out. Why did you hit your old lady, Juan?"

"I found her sleeping with my best friend. She's a cheating bitch you know."

"You two will have a break from each other then."

"What is your immigration status?"

"I'm legal! Got my green card."

"You mean you got an expired card?"

"No sergeant. Everything good with the card."

"I hope so for your case."

William walked out of the room and passed the waiting prisoners and then outside for a cigarette. Normally the questioning would happen the night before the convicts were sent upstate. But the boredom of the job and a vague trepidation of seeing the men's faces led him to conduct the business later than anyone was accustomed. It was already late March but the fallen and blackened snow was frozen solid in four foot mounds along the sidewalk. He didn't hate any of the men he sent upstate, nor did he feel guilty about seeing the group leave, that part of him died a long time ago. William was every bit the prisoner as the ones being led out into the freezing air. He heard the whispers around him from all the other officers.

No one in the station trusted him as no sergeant is trusted in any precinct in New York City or Long Island. He was always going to be the outsider giving orders he knew would surely be ignored. When any of his guys shot a kid down, he felt the noose around his neck tighten as the television stations demanded answers from him. All the while there were forever officers sitting in diners crucifying him as being just another clueless asshole who accepted the hated job of "Sergeant."

"Yeah, the sergeant is a douchebag. Screw that guy, I'm here for a few more months then I'm taking the detective's test. I ain't going to have to listen to that asshole anymore. He thinks he knows what's going on…"

He was too old to take the test himself and he was the only one stupid enough to accept the sergeant's job. So there was nowhere for him to go but retire and that was still five years away. He reached into his pants pocket and pulled out a single cigarette followed by a zippo lighter. He breathed in the first drag, long and slow then exhaled a plume of smoke which dissipated into the gray frozen sky.

William looked around outside the station at the ever changing city. Just outside of view was the diner where he got his first cup of coffee as a rookie. It was later replaced by a Pottery Barn and now was nothing more than an empty store front. Gone too were the white knuckled cops who strong armed the hookers and shook down gang bangers for drugs and money. Now he was surrounded by amateurs, often busting black kids for smoking joints in the parks or clamping down on the homeless and the hopeless who sleep in Penn Station. Many of these kids were brutal meter maids, bringing in anyone when there was a need for overtime or the ennui of boredom became too great.

Gone were the honest payoffs that allowed the professional girls to continue to walk the streets and the police to eat well. All the girls now worked for agencies which advertised in the back of the Village Voice or Chinese massage parlors. Today's police force, William sadly surmised, was on the dollar of landlords of SROs who brought in thugs for hire to clear out their buildings. Many of them (the thugs for hire) had grown used to being residents of boiler rooms where immigration was none the wiser of their presence. He had long grown tired of reading in the papers of the bored brutality committed by cops in the Bronx, Staten Island or Brooklyn. There was hardly a week when a suspect was not shot down in the tenements or found among piles of trash bags. But in the heart of Manhattan, the real estate was as clean as ancient Rome. The outer boroughs became the hinterlands to the great shining city, occupied by the pretty and the immaculate faced children living off of massive trust funds.

William closed his eyes, feeling a migraine coming on. He was greeted by the lightless room that had become all too familiar. There were to be no dreams in this windowless room. Not those which come at night or otherwise. There were no shadows anywhere which came as a mercy. For he feared all shadows for the same reason all cops fear shadows. It is the fear of meeting all those they had a hand in sending upstate; there was the small time pot dealer, the prostitute caught up in a raid and all the youths who enter the system without fangs. What returned were beaten and raped wolves of the penitentiary system. Prison has always been the criminals training camp.

Somewhere a radio was playing. He couldn't tell if it was in the back of his cranium or from some unseen car,

I've got ::cling cling:: fsssss steam heat.

I've got ::cling cling:: fsssss steam heat.

But I need your love to keep away the cold.

I've got ::cling cling:: fsssss steam heat.

I've got ::cling cling:: fsssss steam heat.

I've got ::cling cling:: fsssss steam heat.

But I can't get warm without your hand to hold.

"What kind of old savage bastard could be playing that forgotten goddam song now?" For the pressure building in his head was not unlike the steam that comes through the pipes before leaving the radiators in a hiss. That song was coming from the back of the furthest recess of his mind. William laughed softly, a defeated laugh. The deafening sound of heavy bass and rhythmic ramblings from a passing car drowned out the sound of Williams radio. He opened his eyes to see the last of the prisoners being ushered in on the bus.

He looked up and there high above the city a golden light shone down on him. He knew it was not holy, but neither was he.

"Look!" He cried. "My ship has finally come in."

Untitled

The shades have long been drawn hiding the SRO of the heart
as the hollers of those who lived behind its walls
has been drowned out by
the roar of the traffic
passing through
always just passing through,
or the laughter of the youth
whose trust funds are swollen
but whose souls are vacant
as just another warehoused unit.
It takes real money
an embezzler's money
to walk pretty
along these streets
and forget the ghosts of a city
who now exist only behind the heavy metal door
sleeping the sleep of the forgotten.
Still others haunt the craniums,
like so many flashing images,
of those who were there for the party.
New York use to be the kingdom of misfits
but now sits as the city of those
who will forever be
just visiting.

2

The clocks now measure the movement
of Manhattan
foot by foot
towards being just another museum city
which has a past
but no history.
The shades on those memories have been drawn
they have all become empty store fronts with for rent signs
on silent glass.
The dramas now hide behind those buildings

where the thugs for hire
are the management.
Judges become filing clerks
and the police become armed security
for all the landlords
and the tenants have become
the inmates.
This is the only city that can turn
a meatpacking district into a fashion show
where the shops spring up like
cat-tails in a polluted heart.
This is the death of the union
for those with broad backs
while the beautiful people plant their high heel shoes
in the back of some Guatemalan kid's neck
sewing 50 more garments
in an hour
no exceptions.

There is no town harder on its artists
or moves faster to white wash its history,
sending all its ghosts to wander among the forgotten names
and caskets marketed with serial numbers on Potter's Field
and yellow like forgotten newspapers
in a hoarder's upper west side apartment.

To the Guard Behind the Metal Door: Let Me In!

For Armine

What year is it behind your eyes?
Is your face still young
still in time
like a photograph in the back room
of a hoarder's upper west side apartment?
Last time I saw you
your skin was so white.
Not even the precision of the makeup artist's brush
could hide that blank canvass
where your pigment was lifted.
It was like bleached coral.
Pigment is detail
the eloquence of those continents which you escaped
and shook off into the Coney Island waters
and into the silent screen
during your first double feature.

Do you remember your final farewell to those Polish
nights of your birth as you lay there silent?
The boldness of your voice
permeating every other room
you were ever in
was gone.
It was an amputation
like severed flowers
wilting
somewhere in the back of your throat.

2
The body,
is all that remains
when the bill is due
like a rent demand under
your
door
before ruin sets in.
The eyes become dead cameras.

The ear soon only knows silence.
But when you live in your head
the years all spent
and litter the mind
as vacant words in a recluse's forgotten book,
then gravity never has to
caress your voice
the one which has been stolen
for too long
like a praying mantis sizing up her lover
before devouring him
after his last act of purpose.
Gravity is what left your mouth an empty cave
which even blind catfish will never call a natural home.
Everything you know survives between the sheets
and memories shatter with the most delicate touch.
What is your name
behind those drawn shades
that hides you from the waking world?
Is it necessary
or did that name become a dead limb
now that you've reached the tundra
where there are no more compromises
and all absolutes swallow their own tails
in this
the seasons of your passing
where memories grow pale
thin and delicate
before the final thought is dissolved
like a single piece of paper in the middle of a storm
during
closing night
of
your
show.

Ocean

Have you really dived so far below the waters
of finality's oceans
and
canals and into
that hospital bed
where you were always
just visiting.
There is no need
to come up for air when one likes it better down there.
The years break at the waterline
while
each clock is set to measure
the depths you must reach before you can
no longer
look up to the light
and watch the silhouettes of everyday people
in their everyday cars pass on by without a kind word.
Down here the body is more than just rooms
where evictions notices are always waiting
and the grave is not part of a time share
"Sorry man but we have to move you."
In the subways,
the trains pass by
without any signs of kindness
or collusion
their lights always look to pass through the next tunnel.
They are ghosts of former slaves
trained for decades to
serve without speaking
without connection
to anything permanent.
They know how easy
the voice can become a severed limb
just out of the reach of the camera of need.

These trains carry loveless businessmen
in their loveless cars
to loveless homes.

This is the American prairie
where the Buffalo are insane taxi drivers
looking for a fare to take anyone downtown
refusing to take you
home
uptown
at one in the morning.

For My Mother

One last thought for my mother
who escaped herself
and the confines of the skull
after her operation.
I look for you now
a month after the incision.
You were willing to swim
far below the sheltering light of the surface.
It takes a special metabolism to swim at these depths
(where even most fish disappear or swim above your head)
only to return to one's ruin
or the prison of a body strapped down
in a hospital bed
where the walls have become too familiar.
When did your mind turn back on you
releasing everything that you thought
was left behind
like yellowed newspapers
buried in Potter's Field
and forgotten?
But even the darkest shadows can't hide the imprint
of a mother whose words were designed
in an unwelcomed
winter
to keep you paying the debt
of drudgery
and serving a sentence
in a cranium where there is no time at all
only the endless avenues of the forgotten.

I thought I found you the other day
with the tubes and wires connected to your arms
through your nose and on your fingertips.
It turned out to be a jelly fish
that passed by without acknowledgment or kindness.

Are you moving toward the endless avenues of eternal sleep?
Are you prepared to be consumed by the ward?
A friend of mine escaped from there
before she escaped into finality's ascending ocean.
Or can you tame those indignities
which you thought were dormant
in their rooms far below the water line?

When all the tiny terrors which you have collected run dry
then all that is left behind
in that well
is ruin
and the fear of facing the rest
of your life
as it all comes crashing down on you.
There is only so high
that you can rise
to escape
her
and yourself.
This is your greatest art.
Breaking down
hate
to its purist form
till it takes the shape of a bullet
which always hits its mark
and you find yourself
strapped down in a hospital bed
and spit flying off your lips
as you surrender yourself to another fit
of rage.

Rage is the purist form of hate
and the quickest way to find yourself peering
from the other side of the metal door
which is always locked.

Last time I saw you
your demands became more fierce
"Hurry up we have to get outta here!"
"Go where?"
"There is no where to go."
"I don't know."
"Why do you make cry?"
"Tell me!"

Behind these demands
you were a young girl
still on Long Island or
Brooklyn
waiting in your room
for a letter
which reads
"Body voided recall one last time."
But fate must have changed the number on the door
since the letter has yet to be delivered.

The only escape now
is to placate these indignities
which comes at the cost of a ticket
to the tiny dramas that you have perfected
to a fine art
and now you must forget
or be consumed by those memories.
Don't you realize
that the old man
is waiting for you
on the other side of
those surface waters
of lucidity?
This is no sacrifice that you're going through.
What debt did you think you were paying off
and
what price are you willing to pay?
We must all return to the surface
every once in a while.

4

We spent the day at your bedside
but you had already left the Synagogue of the body
because there was no more room there for you.
The recall of the body came after all.
The landlord of disease came with his notices.
Our flight from New York came too late.
Your leaving came too soon.

5

Were you finally paroled from
The indifferent score keeper of the cross
outside your hospital window
since you've been consumed by
the wasted hours
of endless mornings
which fill all your photo albums
each moment caught in the still frames of
photographs
of winter
and summer
in Brooklyn and Long Island
in its black and white skin?
All the pictures of you
your smiles were false;
the beaten animal of a mother's contempt
that sat behind your eyes like an unwelcomed pet
was true.

Under the silent watch of the GW bridge which I see from 173rd street
I yell to the empty sky
"What plan required you to weep in the time of cancer
and your body sits as lightless ash
under an indifferent sky?"

What plan was left for my father to drown in America
where there is no time to sit Shiva?!

For Ruth

Now that you have reached the forever turning
midnight carousel
which runs on the reel of everything that you know
and waits for no one at all
can you still reach moments of clarity
or have the last strings which you have clung to snapped
and will you disappear into the ocean
painted on the otherwise blank canvass
of the cranium
where there is no gravity
only drifting memories that come in and out of focus
like the last films
of your childhood
Manhattan
Yonkers
and Brooklyn
projected in your vacant theater
Coney Island's last stand.
Will you exist behind an unseen membrane
living in a parallel world to the one you will leave behind?
I know you
in your Jewish skin
which is now translucent
and your descent into midnight.

Do you really wish to escape the family
who now wears the terrifying faces of
familiar strangers
who lurk in the alley ways of all your nightmares?

What you should have known before it was too late
is that it never pays to be so assured
that morning will come again
those unwelcomed mornings
you kept on the other side of your door
or the life you trusted for so long
was tamed and wouldn't turn back on you
like a wolf

like a kept ape
like a hostage bound and gagged
escaping your final act of desperation.

Someone flipped the script on you
as the reception to this program starts to break up
and there is only static now.
Even the memory of your home fades into the final vapor trails
of your Long Island's last gleaming.

The drugs that they force you to swallow
are your last connections to the hours
on this side of the ocean.

This is the fatal flaw on trusting the body as your natural home
when everything breaks down into borrowed time
and there is no need to ask if you can stay
the answer will always be the same
and comes with an eviction notice.
After all
You knew the body will be recalled sooner or later
but until then
boredom and your nurse
that fuckin' nurse will remain your prison guard.
But you were supposed to be just visiting.
No deal could be made
not with prayer
or proposition
to reverse the course of this show you never asked to be in.
But learn to dance in your prison
among those photographs which serve as ghosts
to your private theater
or the hand of bitterness and defeat
will become your hand
then
the
only escape will be diving down
your basement stairs
and death will become your final art.

Forever Turn
The Midnight Carousel

Three Years Too Late

Do you ride with the angels
now that you have consolidated all your tortures
into one
giving you that long inaccessible courage
which you had propositioned
in the allowance
to dive one last time
to reach the end of your line?
I got the news three years too late.
And there is nothing worse than too late
(as one poet said)
or getting the message from a glowing screen.
I know this decision came together
when your mind,
which served a 46 year sentence
in the wards of the cranium,
planned its escape
from your pale body.
It always reminded me of Degas's young models,
white as only the finest porcelain
and smooth.
This last desperate act
could only give birth to the final burlesque
of your tiny torments
that wear the faces born of
sleepless time
where you screamed into the empty space
of mornings that came too soon.
All the clocks have stopped measuring hours
after all
years ago
and became reminders
that sleep comes too late.

You should have realized that you were always the center of this dance.
But this is your finest mistake,
to believe that you can find safety in the darkness of the audience
that you could escape the recoil
of your family's attention.
But you danced freely
the dance of the beautiful
but never forgotten
into the wards
of South Oaks
or attempted to follow your father into the uncharitable depths of
alcohol's cruel ocean.

I saw you in the photograph.
Your eyes were two empty rooms
in a vacant home.
You were already gone.
I know your tears had become fatal
then
and washed you away into that gray sea
where you made all your future plans.

Merry
did you ever consider staying in the lighted room
where all your demons hide in their muted discourse?
Perhaps then you could have tasted
one last time
those droplets of Steve Forbert's bitter words of love
which you swore were meant for you.

Escape
that's just theater.
That's just mind games which you will always lose
in your last attempts
to proposition your free fall
that ends with the tightening of the rope.
I know
your final performance (and the rope)

were meant to cut off the source of the pain
because that's where the demons were born
and that's where the genius
of your madness
and desperation became as one.
Perhaps if you didn't
cast yourself to the silent winds
of each lovers promises
which you formed into a bullet designed for eternal sleep,
then
perhaps you wouldn't
have ended
your final show
in ruin.
If you hadn't traced the outline of this fate
in Pilgrim
or South Oaks
then perhaps you would have embraced those stray moments of happiness
that took the form of felines rubbing against your heels
which they know as home.
The currency of your fatality
has no change
only the pain of being spent.

This is the last thing I hand over to you
the song of you
that exudes the scent of honeysuckle
the same as the shampoo and perfume
you wore.
Each word contains the taste of you
that resides in my memories
like ghosts in a museum of not so ancient artifacts.
But I don't have the strength
or the voice
to conduct the performance,
to give this song the attention that it deserves.
What you deserved.

For that
you would need to learn to tame the Hudson River
or learn the art of losing well.
This music
still reverberates in your name
like phantom echoes
from an unseen radio
in an otherwise empty avenue
of another sleepless night
and
every street
leads
back
to you.

If you learned to breathe under the smothering sky
with its weight that reminds us how easy it is to be crushed
by foul things and failed decisions
which yellow like newspapers on the bottom of piles
of a hoarder's upper Westside apartment
then perhaps you could have found a home
beyond the promises of all the jokers
and into a body that never turns
its back on you.

The Ghost

Am I a ghost in your eyes?
In your cranium?
In your neighborhood?
In the smoke of the cigarettes of strangers who line the sidewalk:
you used to walk
or in your thirst for those waters of the storming and gray seas
which you looked into
cutting off all future plans
of walking in the unwelcomed morings?
Or am I just a finger print on your front window
which is dark now that you're gone?
I still stagger through your waves
to find you in your upstairs apartment
out on Long Island
in this
your final show
the exit of your last design
and your escape from the undertow
that was dragging you down
since you were sixteen
when you danced among birth control pills
or the ward's cold embrace.
You were never going to be part of the afterhours scene
wading through those mornings which came too soon
and yellowed by the torment
of a father who dove into alcohol's cruelest ocean.
I knew you before the sound engulfed your streets.
Even then your tongue was devastated.
All your words became as downed trees from an unfelt wind
scattered and reversing course every time you spoke
wishing you could escape your body and leave your name behind.
What remained was the bitter pain
of finding your final cries replaced
by death's serrated laughter.
Even tears lose their silent voice
sooner or later.

And all the good times are now just flickering projections
on your far nocturnal wall
always moving in slow motion
as if the collapse of everything you trusted was deliberate
and always seemed to belong to someone else
anyone else
who knows the art of being fucked over
and surviving
well
as if all you ever knew was this eternal night that your skin
seemed to fit so well
with a hunger that
never could be denied.

Did you think you were going to be forgotten,
as if you were a strange and obscure idol consumed by the ever ascending
wilderness shrouding you in vines and the honeysuckle which permeated
from your hair?
Surrender
that is the price of living in the night of the silent snow
and a soul on the take
for the treasures of a lesser majesty.
You were never going to leave your ruin to anyone else
or lend your escape to chance
as if it was your finest touch at the end of your finger tips.
The snap of that rope fastened around your throat
was to make sure
to
cut that source off with the fierce kindness of gravity.
The light that flashed before your eyes
was no station
but was
every one of your cries
your screams
and the season of the wards
becoming as one in the supernova of what once was.

But Merry
in your waking hours which came
from being up far too long
did you ever consider finding a home
in the lighted room
where all your friends still gather
in your name
and where your cats still sit as witnesses to that fateful morning?

Dancing in Two Worlds

What drawn shades do you dance behind
now that you escaped your mother's house
for a more distant tenement?
Does your voice still whisper
with the steam
that passes through the pipes
as if the radiator was a confessional
or an operator connecting a long distance call?

2
Why did you swim from the boat
in the painting
above the bedroom mirror
racing just beyond my call
towards the open sea
and cry that there was no one there to save you from drowning?
You should have looked behind you one more time
and known that there is nothing at the end
of those waters?
Or
did you think you'd join the sisterhood of mermaids
with their sinister smiles and angry laughter?
They,
like
you,
prefer to be lost at sea
than be a prisoner
in another man's narrow stare.

Their rejection which comes
sooner or later
only lead to endless nights
and failed connections.

You embraced the last gleaming of your voice
which you swallowed with all those pills
that were supposed to be the key

to the first attempt at escaping.
It was a trick perfected with motives and tears.
They told me you turned your doctor into an accomplice
in the felony of escaping
all the mornings
that were never supposed to come.
You had taken the form of another politician
and she another blind voter.
You learned the art of the twisted promise
after
all.
You did it better than any man
or dollar store joker who smiled your way.
Each word became a felony.
Your course
and intent
meant the end
of your crooked line.
Lines.
That's what you knew
as you sailed into the gray sea
of all future plans.

And
your laughter and assurance
to her
that you'd live another day
became serrated and cut deeper than
your feline embrace would allow.

And
now all that remains is silent tension below the tree
in your brother's back yard
that you call home.

But Merry
I'd like to spit into the gray dust that was your mouth
so perhaps

you can taste
even for a moment
black coffee and the sweet honeysuckle
that permeated your hair
or to dance under the sheltering sky.

You swore that you could never
reach those speeds
to outrun
the demands that gravity
makes on the body.
You tried
to tame your perfect skin
which was so pale
and white
it was as if you traded in the sun
for a life of setting each and every day
reeling
into the winter of the wards
which sits in the skull
where all your screams become as one
and pointed inwards
like a gun
always pressed against a bitter heart
that beat in time
as if every clock
dragged you into those mornings
as a mockery to your indignities.
Do you still waltz with ghosts
among your mother's forgotten things
which now lie in a local landfill
like an homage to all your hate?
You collected all those promises made by so many lovers
all leading to ruined cities
and tears for what they took

and never left behind.
I know you sewed those tears together to form a hair shirt
you claimed would wear
away all those indignities
of being born too late
or too early.

You knew
that this was going to be the closing night
for your show of shows
and when the applause died down
all that would remain
was the reverberation
of your frantic mind
and the promise of your escape
which came in the form of a ticket
to ride the last train
away from the tyranny of time.

Gray Dust

Did you know our lungs
yours and mine
sit as otherwise empty vessels
where the air has been evicted
replaced by the gray exhaust and fluid
of staying too long?
It was as if they (our lungs) were vacant rooms
taken over by someone who was just visiting.
In midtown
forget the inhaler
you still have to breathe the air
with its unforgiving skin and metallic weight
that moves across the tongue as I cough up
what the bridge and tunnel crowd leave behind.
How can you make a natural home in the emergency room
after all our fortunes have been spent
and there are no more deals to cheat the gravity that draws us
from wasted hours at the movies
where we watch as spectators
who sit silently under drawn shades of the darkened theater
to witness the brutality of a projected life
which ends every two hours
only to start over
at
the next show
when all the mistakes sit as an ever present threat
and the end seems certain
and has curdled?
But when the lights come back on
and the thoughts of the body reform
we lose ourselves in the barracks of our clothing
which we give no thought
when picking out each morning.

2
I will never pass as a ghost into the gray dawn's early light
only to return in the afternoon and wait on 8th Ave
for a taxi that never stops.
Nor will my voice only exist in the exhaust of idling cars
but my name will give the gray ash that was your body
the moisture of a life you cried to escape
before you reached
the end of your line
that fateful morning.
And
the mold that has formed around my tub
will claim a piece of my last breath.
Something you should know
my breath is not modern
it is a relic
which I keep on a shelf in my bedroom
by the air conditioner
where it is allowed to flow
and form the shape of words
you will never hear.

Walking in Central Park with You

I want to walk through Central Park with you
not as lovers
I'm suddenly too young for that
now that your distance is far too great.
Even when we were in bed together you were two feet away
but miles out of reach.
That distance was always going to take
the form of a
straight
razor
which you used to cut away your gravity
so you could drift through those waters of the gray seas
of all your future plans.
Its 11:38 in midtown Manhattan
as I write you this letter
and already my thoughts of you
have come in on the waves of my fear and trepidation
which is usually kept at low tide by Prozac.
Your ghost is always white as a snow drift
not in New York
where all the snow is black from the passing cars
or the latest construction work.
More like Washington State or Minnesota or Germany
where they do a better job hiding their excesses.
Its not so unlike being at our apartment on Lehigh St
where you needed to be held tightly
with your head pressed firmly against my shoulder.
It's true that the taste of coffee was not enough to keep you around.

I wanted to watch your movements in the grips of troubled sleep
more than any film noir
shown at 3 in the morning.
But you should have known that the body is borrowed and never owned.
It's a rental with no option to buy.
We are only visiting after all.
And where did you think you were going to land
before being shit out by the wards?

Did you really believe that you were a saint
or think that you could tame the ascending wilderness
which you feared would consume the idol of your name?
It's a greater trick than taming your own perfect skin
or claiming your body as your own.
Those anti-depressants could have kept your indignities
at low tide
before you embraced that fateful morning when you reached the end
of your line.

2

Those flames of the incinerator licked your perfect skin and hair
as your body lay in the shadows of ruin
which you perfected as an art form
or a well planned assault.
I still think of the gray dust that replaced your beauty.
Did you think that you were going to get an applause
after your silent exit
or did you feel cheated
out of the life
you swore was just around the corner
but never showed?
Those flames sent up smoke signals letting us know
that you finally knew when to leave.
That was your great escape
to avoid living the encircled life of a shut-in.
Rooms after all can become wombs of
dry wall and concrete
if you stay too long.
And the flicker of the television set where you wept
for Doctor Quinn or Touched By An Angel
became too bright
and your morning was never meant to come.

The Last Ode

Merry did you ever fear
that your words would fall into the black snow of the city
of sleep
and curdle,
until the ice melts and washes out into the Hudson
only to feed the fish and eels
and night crabs and all other foul things
that live among the chemicals from upstate
and garbage that settled on the bottom of that river
far below where any light could reach?
Each letter
each word will only be shit out into the sewage
of all your indignities
and flushed out into the deserted sea.
Why didn't you embrace the SRO of the heart
where you could hide in the bathroom
down the soulless hall?
Perhaps then you could have known all your cheated hours
not as enemies
but as equals
or roaches
depending if the lights are on or off.
Your age is a lie,
You are always going to be a little girl
crying into the side of time.
That's where you will find all your regrets
as they turn and sneer.
And
trying to convince your audience
that you broke the ennui like a horse
or a pet wolf
turning it into a pearl which you roll around with your tongue
right behind your teeth
that's just the boredom of advertising.

2

I must admit that I looked through
our albums
filled with pictures of you and me and
I wonder
what emergency hides behind your smile?
What grin sent you spiraling down
ever deeper into uncharted depths
where not even the most potent drugs
could drag you back to the surface.
But you should have learned how to navigate its waters.
Do you understand?
Those are not cats waiting for you on the other side
of your door.
Nor is it a savior
whose blood touches your lips
like milk pouring into the mouth of a babe
on the end of her mother's tit.
That's my gravity claiming all of your confessions
with their vicious nature designed to
cut off all your connections
beyond the heavy metal door
or in the mornings that come too soon
so perhaps you can dive
one last time
into the sleep of the forgotten.
Your tongue is not a church
despite using guilt as a cross
to drive all your fortunes
into
roach hotels
where there is no escape
only television sets and the recycled air of shut-ins.

You should have known that
living in your body is not a felony
you are hardly Chinatown.
I'd like to play your vocal chords
to perhaps find the right note
and
cut through the feedback of all your regrets
and bend that note to a sweeter music.

Merry's Last Gleanings

I want to lay my head across your chest
to hear your heart beat
to know you are still alive.
But your chest and its heart are now gray ash
dry as ancient bedrock
where oceans of tears once flowed under the light
of a lamp that sat on your night stand
and the flicker of the television set.
You were never going to live behind the heavy metal door.

Did I say live?
There is no life in the wards
only the cold and pale skin of existing.
You were never again going to stumble in that blue gown
with the tag around your wrist.
Did the Christ born of the needle's prick dessert you
like all the others
and no longer answer your prayers which came in like radio static
exuded from the tongue
before the sedative found its mark
and cast you into the dreams
of someone who finds a natural home
in states of emergency?
Your voice should have been a radio.
Then you could have turned to the right station
and found the Rock N' Roll of the heart.
I would like to put all the moisture
back into the earth that was your body.
Not with water but with coffee
black of course.
Any source of life should be uncut
by milk or water.
Then perhaps the serrated edges of your words
will no longer be dulled.
Bitterness does become a swollen
gland if left untreated.

That is why I'm writing you this letter
at 4:45 AM
after a night of no sleep
after a long string of insomniac nights
to let you know that pills could have plugged the broken dam
that carried you away
only to flow into the winter
where the muted and blind snow weeps silently
now that you're gone.

Last Turn of the Morning Carousel/
Forever Turn the Midnight Carousel

Birthday Poem for Merry

Am I just another antiquity?
An artist who finds a natural home
Among the paupers whose graves are marked with serial numbers
Instead of headstones?
I hate gimmicks and dismiss them
like any other moment of mediocrity.
The truth is
that I have no problem
with standing among broken things
(Which have lost their lacquer
along with most of the pigment
born of memory).
Memories
and the past are bombed out cities
with many blind allies
and dead ends
along with the hustlers of our wishful thinking
who makes everything we recall as unreliable as the New York Post.
So why do we rely on this memory
or anything else which is expedient with its answers?
You should know
I live
just on the outskirts of any post war city of memory.
For that's the last place I can find you
still smiling in rare moments of being among
friends without pretense
and those who you felt knew too well of the
fits
and fury which you failed to tame
with its fatal recoil.
And you use that wind to start another
storm,
fragile as a little girl one moment
then

fierce as the wards the next.
I would like to take the gun that has been pressed against your heart
since you were 16
and turn it onto the demons that you hunted to escape
with pills
and boyfriends
and expedited answers from Long Island gurus
so perhaps we can live ordinary lives
with ordinary fears of everyday things.
We can write letters of discontent to the New York Times
or find a home in banality.
You should have known that I've
grown tired of keeping company with artists.
Their conversations
and their letters have become fatally urgent
crying about the end of this long running party
we know as civilization.
Oh how I would love to spend one more afternoon in bed with you
watching TV or listening to music.
I could hold you again
and you could think of my arms as a beach
emptied of all the people
so you could skinny dip in the welcoming waters freely.
The waves could wash away
South Oaks
and Pilgrim
into a feverish dream of
straps on the bed
and clocks that announce med time.
I'd always keep a pot on for you.
I'd love to have taken a candle
to burn away that mark
that no x ray would ever find.
Who knew that its roots
could reach so far beyond your years
keeping your most vile anxieties
alive
and well

or intertwine
your words
your phrases
which
you have sculpted into tiny ships
to sail you
away from here.
Did those roots
drag you into those
mornings which came too soon
while waiting for the promises of a midnight
which never came at all.
If only you didn't follow those demons to the rope's end.
Then perhaps the candle I'll light for you tomorrow wouldn't burn all
night
your breath could have taken care of that.
But what remains guarantees the last turn of the morning carousel
and forever turns the midnight carousel.

Oh September

Oh September
I found your brutal heart
with its endless winds of an early winter.
Oh how I would have protected you
from that September of the fateful year 2009
to all the Septembers until you and I meet once again Merry
in an otherwise empty and indifferent room
where there are no scorekeepers
to call the game.
If you can own a judge in housing court
for the right price
or the right position
then why can't you own the scorekeepers as well?
And who is keeping score on them?
Are our worn souls
those of us faithful losers
really worth so much that we can't be forgotten?
Oh Merry maybe I just should be angry with you
leaving no letter behind
or a phone call explaining why all your tomorrows have been recalled
as if your bill owed to no one at all
was just too great
to pay off.
Didn't you know we could have danced
like children in all our ruins?

Your avenues have become vacant.
And your cars have all stopped.
Your city has become a ghost town
in September's white out.
Even those who lived there are now evicted from all memory.
And all the score keepers have called the game
indifferent to the cheated soul that still stands
abandoned in your vacant streets,
and loveless like a house cat looking out the window
on to a world it knows it will never be a part of again.
Who rings in your absence?

Behind the Heavy Metal Door

The heavy metal door closed behind Ann Horn as she was ushered along by an orderly and a male nurse. The echo of the door's closing vibrated in her head, worsening a migraine which came by way of vomiting up a bottles worth of sleeping pills. She could barely keep her eyes open; the harsh light of the ward gave her the feeling that her headache had become a laser beam shooting through her skull.

The antiseptic smell of cleaning solution permeated the air reminding everybody around, both patient and doctor alike, that as long as they were in there, they were now severed from the outside world as if they were even for a short time, ghosts in a timeless mission. Ann started to laugh a defeated laugh, at the thought of a portcullis slamming down in front of the metal door.

"We're in a lunatic kingdom," she mumbled to herself, still in a state of delirium. They passed an old black man standing in the middle hallway holding up his beltless pants with one hand and stroking the light while demanding everyone in sight accept him as being the one true god.

"Great we now have four 'Gods' on this floor" the male nurse joked to the orderly. "One of the others was picked up last night after he was found on 23rd street, tearing pages out of a Bible and eating them. Poor bastard just kept shouting that he was eating the flesh of his son." Both laughed as an act of routine.

They reached a waiting a room where Ann collapsed onto a plastic chair placed in front of a desk. Off to the right an empty chair was placed for any doctor willing to conduct the questioning. "Wait here, the doctor will be here in a few minutes" the orderly told Ann Horn flatly. The two men walked out of the room and disappeared around the corner.

Now alone, Ann realized her body continued to shake uncontrollably as her breath came in gasps and lightheaded daydreams. Images passed by of electric storms followed by a thousand slamming metal doors which sounded like jackboots marching at midnight. She blooded her hands beating on each door, screaming "let me back in!" Each remained sealed shut. But for just a moment each thought gave her the comfort of a prisoner who just achieved escape from the penitentiary of the body and disappeared over the horizon. Around every corner was the promise of the final box car pulling out of the station just in time for her to jump on and reach her final destination. But the police and her doctors somehow always knew when to unravel their flypaper to catch her in mid-stride. Every time they bring her back, they seem to tighten the screws a little more to lock her in the prison of each morning. Each attempt at escape usually ended with her hanging from the wall, with the spot lights and machine guns pointed at her back. Her decisions were always the same, to haul herself across the wall and dare the guards to shoot her from behind or fall into the court yard and go to work the following morning as if nothing ever happened. Ann never wore the face of indifference though, for any boyfriend or occasional lover. They all wound up in the oncoming storm of tears and resentment towards their love and that they dared to stick around for too long. But she could never be alone for too long before she made another run for the wall. She always took the "coward's way out" in the end and dropped into the court yard. It was these fantasies that made her to want to escape even more. The antiseptic reek of cleaning fluid was heavy in the air acting as a reminder that she failed once again.

There was a loud crash from somewhere near, coupled with the terrified screams of an unseen woman. Ann got up slowly to look out the door. She braced herself against the wall as she walked towards the hallway as her legs were still shaking and her balance had been severed. Her eyes were still partly closed as her headache had only gotten worse. Even in her haze she had a need to watch the commotion but saw nothing. All the noise came from behind a closed door three rooms down. Before long the door opened and two nurses wheeled out a pretty, pale skinned girl with long blond hair which covered her face. The girl was strapped down to a hospital bed not uttering a word but just stared off into the distance far out of the reach of the wards. She had been drugged, that was clear as she was too incapacitated to walk, lying silent and still. The girl's blue gown ended at her ankles and shoeless feet. For a moment, Ann wondered what the girl's story was but couldn't focus enough to maintain her curiosity. The feeling of being sick had started rising from somewhere deep below and was now stuck in her throat. She moved back to her seat and collapsed. Her body became slack except for her jaw which remained clenched from the pain of the blinding light which seemed to force her eyes closed. She realized her body was no longer shaking as before, only her left arm trembled a bit. All the noises around her came in waves which seemed to be getting further and further away until they were nothing more than echoes. The light from the room invaded the last places which she had grown accustomed to fleeing into, preventing any chance of escaping from the wards. Ann strained to look up and peered around the room as if she were hunting for something specific but the room was all but empty except for two chairs and the desk which she sat in front of.

Any suicide case would be safe from themselves here, no wires to hang themselves or sharp edges on the desk. The door sat wide open with passing nurses looking in as they moved like fish in a bowl. The room was awash in white, painfully white which emphasized the lifelessness of the space that came as a reminder of how separated the outside world truly was from the universe behind the heavy metal door. It was in Ann's mind, a death which was worse than any natural passing. Here, there were no mornings, afternoons or nights. The clocks only kept track of med time, dinner time and bed time. Everything in between was empty time, where one could wander the hallways or lose themselves in their rooms. Even the years were prohibited from passing through the heavy metal door. All of those who were awake were themselves, ghosts of those who had never truly died at all but only visiting the world of the forgotten. Everyone in the ward, both staff and ghost alike, seemed to move or scream or look around offices and padded rooms as if there was no outside world at all.

Then there were the lucky ones, those who claimed the few windows in the place as their own, keeping their connection to the outside world alive. There was not a man or woman among this lot who cared if they were let back out on to the street or kept locked up. It all seemed the same somehow. They would just stare outside as the passers-by rushed as if they were late and would always be late no matter what time appeared on the clocks or watches. But for the lucky ones looking down on the bleached sidewalks of the Upper East Side, returning to the outside world meant collecting soda cans which were used to fill garbage bags until they hit the deposit machines. The money from the cans and bottles went towards one dollar slices of pizza or the cheapest hit of whatever was available. Still others saw the wards as a way out of sleeping under the bridges of Hell's Kitchen where one was always prepared to defend themselves against attacking rats the size of kittens, some much bigger. For all of them though, the world on the other side of the bars was a terrifying wilderness where they themselves were the hunted. The hunters, who never seemed far behind the game, were the demons born of headlights from the oncoming cars, street lights from Hudson River Park or the roar of the subway cars.

It was all about passing the time between taking meds and being sent to their rooms. Some took to leaning their time away along the walls next to the windows. While others burned their time away screaming at invisible assailants. But the luckiest ones of all weren't those who stood behind the barred windows looking down on the city, but those who were passed out in their beds unaware of any windows or outside world or even the wards themselves. These vegetables would forever run through the empty streets of drugged sleep, away from the demons, the nurses, the police and the pimps. The yearless avenues were now theirs alone as much as any silent suffering had been since the streets and jail cells rose up to greet them.

Just outside the door, a tall Jewish kid with a yarmulke stood looking blankly down the hall, "the machine in my head doesn't work, nothing works. The machine in my head doesn't work, nothing works. I've been here for seventy years and nothing works. The machine in my head doesn't work, nothing works…" A young nurse approached the young man, asking if he knew what was the matter. The kid just stared off into a void speaking a little louder. "The machine in my head doesn't work, I've been here for seventy years. Nothing works. The machine in my head doesn't work. Nothing works."

Ann's eyes fell closed again. For the first time since the fateful hour when she tried to swallow all of her meds at the same time, she realized the dull pain in her stomach. It was not so unlike the early signs of a toothache. It seemed to somehow merge with her migraine which was starting to return to a new peak. The kid's endless rambling reached deep into the beating behind her eyes as her hands tightened into two fists and her nails dug deep into her palms. The voice of a second nurse urged the kid to calm down or he would have to be put back into "the quiet room." Without having to look up Ann could hear all three walk down the hall while the kid's voice began to become more distant.

The door to the room closed lightly. Ann looked up with some surprise. He was a short Indian man, with olive skin and a salt-and-pepper beard which failed to hide the fact that he was still young. Despite showing an understanding smile, his face lacked all warmth somehow. It was as if the smile was issued by management along with the name tag over his left coat pocket. Even his eyes had an institutional deadness to them. He slowly sat in the chair next to the desk with a clipboard in hand. The doctor leaned forward as the smile vanished from his face. He began to speak with a heavy accent and the reassuring tone of a grandmother.

"You are a lucky woman to be alive Ms. Horn. I know it doesn't feel that way at the moment having just come here from the emergency room and all. You must be exhausted since it is nearly four in the morning. But please understand this is all necessary to find out what is going on with you. Another hour could have meant your life. Yes I know that was your goal, best laid plan if you will, but we will see what we can do for you. Maybe make you feel at least, able to cope with whatever you are going through. Medicine has come a long way over the years you understand? I see in your records the last time you were in a hospital the doctor had you on some heavy medication. Yes those type of pills do make you walk around like a zombie. I will do my best to keep you off that drug. Says here you have stopped taking them long ago. Our protocol is far more precise I sure you. "

The doctor read Ann's records slowly line by line to himself, not looking at Ann as if he expected her to crack and confess to a murder case which had never been solved. Ann just looked down at the desk without uttering a word. It was a routine she perfected in evading any attempt by those who she felt would keep her from reaching her final solution. She had taken to ignoring most of the phone calls she would receive in during the evening hours. She would lift up the receiver then hung up. On the other end of the receiver were friends she had once loved and spent the holidays with or volunteered with at a local animal hospice in the middle of a Long Island suburb, or even babysat for when she was much younger. But now they were all enemies whom she kept on the other side of the gate.

"How dare they try to invade my space? Why don't they leave me alone?" But there was never anyone around to answer. Her guilt had long become a loyal friend never leaving her side. When all her boyfriends had walked out the door, or during the loss of an elder cat, the guilt was always was there, never far behind. It was as common to her as it was to every good Catholic. In her head was a record which played the voices of all her regrets and bitter defeat. Most of the time it was her father who had long sunk to alcohol's cruelest ocean before giving way to cancer. Ann had been sure she could have found a way to save him but was never quite sure now. All she knew was she had to be punished like any other good Catholic. Despite this, she never saw herself as a martyr or some remote idol but just a woman in torment looking to pay the bills on a home she could ill afford and to maintain a life that was never truly hers to begin with. When the fits ebbed, she would just grab the remote control and watched tv until the morning's light greeted her. Her elder cat would jump onto her bed and settled down. "Oh Randy, you and I will fall apart together", she gave out a halfhearted laugh then fell asleep.

The doctor looked up from the papers slowly as if he were conniving some dramatic affect. "Says here you were sent to Pilgrim when you were twenty one. That was your first attempt. Nineteen eight five you cut your wrists with a box cutter. Do you have anything to say Ms. Horn?"

Ann continued you sit staring at the desk in silence. The doctor looked back down at the paper then continued.

"It says here your father died and something about a relationship breaking up, both in 85."

This time he didn't look up but just waited for a reply but none came.

"Can you tell me the reason for the break up Ms. Horn?"

"Your father, it says, died of cancer connected to his drinking. Does any of this sound familiar to you?"

How long could she remain silent before she finally broke from being locked up for the mandatory seventy-two hours? It was no secret that she was in a soccer/football match with the doctor. One with no time clock. Ann could play defense for minutes, hours, days or even weeks but sooner or later they were going to score on her and get the information they were looking for. Only a novice would believe otherwise.

The spiraling depression which led her to swallowing herself years ago and the pills that night came flooding back in. She knew there was no way she could last in her private room where there were no doctors at all; so she let out in a voice just over that of a whimper, "yes." She grew silent once more despite knowing that there was no use trying to wait all of them out, it was all a joke she was going to play on herself. She was there on a suicide watch and the outside world would have to wait longer for her return, not really missing her at all. She was, after all not a girl foolish enough to believe that all she had to do was hold her breath and they would let her out or pray to a heaven that was absent of any score keeper.

The doctor didn't look up but waited for a further response. When there wasn't one he continued.

"According to your records Ms. Horn you were unresponsive during your other visits to the hospital." "This is not acceptable of course. You are here, as you know, because you have a serious problem that we need to resolve. We can play the waiting game all you want but you will only prolong your time with us."

This time the fatherly tone disappeared from the doctor's voice seeing he was not getting anywhere playing the good cop. He began to speak with a hardened tone which came as a warning. Ann knew very well the routine of these interrogations. They all started off playing the same concerned parent role but wound up speaking with the same cold voice of the institutions. But despite all she knew, the dam began to break and the waters began to leak through the growing cracks.

"What do you want me to say? We both know you can only hold me for a few days then I'm no longer your concern! You don't care unless I'm locked up here so stop this concerned father bullshit!"

The doctor spoke again without looking up from his clip board, "Tell me about the break up with your boyfriend."

Now exhausted Ann knew there was no use fighting any further, "He lied to me ok? He began buying things we couldn't afford behind my back like this go-cart which he tried to hide at his friend's house! He just stopped telling me things until we did nothing but fight! I slept with his best friend a few times then that was it! We broke up!"

Each word began to come between sobs. "I'm a bad person ok. I'm always hurting someone. I just want to die - but no, I just go on living."

She cried as her head just hung down as if it was that of a marionette whose strings had been cut as the words she tried to speak only disappeared.

"Well Ms. Horn we will talk later when you can speak and you can get ahold of yourself. Right now we will get nowhere. A nurse will be here soon to take you to a room where you will be observed around the clock. Perhaps then you'll calm down so we can dig much deeper and find out the best way to help you. Maybe get you re-tethered if you will. You will be here for a little while so we have time to get to the bottom of things."

"You think they will be able to fix me? They tried this same shit at South Oaks and Pilgrim. I've taken their drugs and went to their therapy and it's a safer bet to depend on blind pigs finding truffles under the driest rock than finding the cure for me. " She thought. She raised the gown sleeve of her right arm, grimaced at its whiteness and visible veins, then put the sleeve back down.

The doctor stood up and walked out of the room. Ann just sat there crying and shaking as each tear dropped on her flowered night gown. Somewhere in the miasma of noise from the wards a kind voice was barely able to cut through, "Let me take you to your room dear. You can talk to the doctor more tomorrow." When she looked up Ann saw that the nurse was looking down on her with huge black eyes with the earnestness of a concerned mother. The nurse's dark skin was a deep contrast to the unbearable whiteness that had been beating on her since she arrived.

Ann wiped her eyes on the back of her gown sleeve while the nurse grabbed her other arm to help her up. The two walked down the hallway past bared windows. Through the blur of her tears, Ann could only see the backs of the patients who did nothing but stand in front of these windows and stare down on the world all day and yet seemed to see nothing at all. The bright blue of late morning, formed a glow around them, giving them the appearance of holy idols.

"Maybe one of 'em is my guardian angel and will save me from all this." Ann thought for a brief second but the feeling of hope quickly turned to bitterness. "How typical even my guardian angel has turned his back on me."

They passed the Jewish kid who now sat in a padded room behind a locked door. The young man just stared blankly. One of three "Gods" of the ward's floor was being escorted to his room screaming scripture at the top of his voice "and you will know my name is the Lord!"

"Come on your holiness" one of two orderlies laughed while dragging the thin and frail patient who had decided not to stand on his own but whose feet were now dragging along the floor.

The nurse guided Ann through a maze of corridors, passing rooms with doors opened or closed. Some were vacant while others were occupied by those sleeping the sleep of the forgotten. In one room an older man slept mercifully unaware of his surroundings. The nurse poked Ann, who had stopped crying and was able to gather her defenses once again.

"Those are one of the lucky ones" the nurse joked. "I wish I could dream myself out of this place" her voice trailed off. "But still, at least we don't have to deal with the winter here. It seems to get too damn cold in February these days and the summer forget it. It is brutal out there. I can't see how anyone could stand it".

"Yea but you miss the fall and spring when everything comes alive."

"That is strange coming from a girl like you. Trying to kill yourself and not wanting any part of this world."

"I don't want any part of living in this body" Ann corrected her "It's so fucking old and ugly. Besides I can still recognize the beauty of the passing seasons which is one reason I'd never live in the city. Just because I'm stuck here doesn't mean I'm completely crazy."

"Please girl you are what? Thirty-four and still pretty. A little pale, yes, and some gray in your head but not old. Wait till you find out what real age is about. And we don't use the term crazy around here dear, some of the guys don't like it. "

There was no answer. For Ann had long decided to settle the debt of drudgery of being sentenced to that body. A few rooms down a woman moved from spot to spot mumbling something about being tracked by the CIA. They continued down, past the day room where bodies were gathered around a television set watching a soap opera through static.

"I wonder if it even matters if there was no picture on the screen at all or if they were forced to watch some stupid cartoon," Ann thought as she mumbled each word separately as if one had no real connection to the other.

"What was that dear?" the nurse asked.

"Nothing just thinking something to myself."

As they moved towards the last room on the left, a short heavy woman walked out from an open door just to the right. The woman was older and toothless with jagged scars across her face, long brown hair fell across her eyes. The blue gown which she wore covered her legs to the knees and did nothing to hide the thick black hair which covered her legs and formed mats down to her ankles.

The woman looked up to Ann, "you got a quarter lady?"

"No I have nothing on me."

The woman looked down with disappointment, "then fuck you,' then walked away.

The nurse stared at Ann with embarrassment but with no sign of surprise in her voice. "I'm so sorry. That's Lucy. She does that everyone here even the staff. She got that habit of asking for money at Willow Brook and some of the guys gave it to her."

When they finally reached the windowless room Ann saw that it was all but empty. There were two beds placed along either side, against the walls one across from each other. Both had thin blankets and sheets and heavily worn pillows. On the bed closest to the door there were some books and a CD walkmen with a few stray disks.

"Your bed is the one on the right dear, this one belongs to Janet. A very nice woman but can be a bit of a bully when she has her fits. She is hardly ever in here, she spends most of her time in the day room. You must have seen her, she was watching TV when we passed."

Ann could not recall anyone who she saw in that day room. They all seemed to be faint images haunting the place. But she was too tired to argue and so wandered over to her bed and laid down. "Someone will be right in dear to speak to you". Ann didn't hear the nurse's parting words. Though she wasn't asleep her mind was a million miles away, in the world beyond the pain and the wards and her family whom she felt regretted her being born in the first place. She was long convinced that they had hoped for a second son, but got her instead. The joke, Ann believed, was on both her family and her. It had long explained why her brother had been the golden child. It was her father though that she felt closest to. He would come home drunk so often, she would yell at him. By morning, the old man remembered nothing.

Her body was too tense to fall asleep despite the increasing gravity of being awake. She found herself listening to all the noise from outside her room. Across the hall a young woman was crying that her family wished she was a boy and didn't care about her. The voice continued to cry out about having to put herself to bed when she was just five years old, about coming into the living room to remind her parents to come in and check on her. Another voice, this of a young man, could be heard bellowing how no one loved him and he wished everyone would stop bullshitting him. Somewhere down the hall she could hear heavy sobbing but couldn't tell if it was a man or a woman. It sounded more like a child's cry which came from the depths of a thousand years of indignities. Only those who knew true defeat could let out a cry like that for there was no greater enemy then the coming of morning. But the cry only came through in a strange static

It was then that Ann realized, with great shock that all the noises she was hearing were coming from inside her head and not the hallway at all. It was if a radio with a strange reception was on high volume. With the realization of the source of the noise, came sudden silence. She sat up for a moment to listen for any sounds from the halls but she could only hear the squeaking wheels of the orderly's cart followed by the clanging of the steam pipes which came as a precursor to the loud hiss of wet heat from the radiators. There was not even a hint or rumor of the television in the day room. Ann thought it strange that the heat was on since it was late March. The last thing she remembered coming in and out of the ambulance was the slow rhythmic sound of water droplets falling from window sills and landings onto the metal railing. She could hear water flowing from her front door stoop and the stairs. The air was getting warm but there was still a hint of a chill in it. She lay back down and stared at the dropped ceiling. There were was yellowed stained above her which reached all the way to the room's overhead light.

Before she could lose herself on the meaning of the stain another nurse came in while being accompanied by the wheels of a cart. "Ms. Horn please sit up I must go over a few things with you. This a routine that we have to do with all our patients."

Ann sat up part of the way resting on her elbow. A heavily built nurse who seemed unnaturally pale stood over Ann. Ann guessed that the woman's colorless complexion must have been the result of spending so many hours in the buzzing neon light, as if she had evolved from some strange creature who could only survive in the environment of the wards. Her hair was a light shade of blond and pulled back in a tight bun. The nurse held two cups, one in each hand. Under her right arm was a blue gown sealed in plastic, along with slippers.

The nurse looked down with two blue disapproving eyes. "As I'm sure you've been told, Ms. Horn, you're on twenty four hour suicide watch while you're here. That means that you must be supervised at all times. When there are no nurses around to look in on you, you must be in the day room. If you go to the bathroom there must be someone there to supervise you. If you have a fit or outburst we reserve the right to strap you down. A nurse will speak to you later about trying different medications to help you get better. I have slippers and a gown here for you to wear and since you've gotten no sleep I brought you something to help you relax."

Ann sat up, swung her legs over the side of the bed. Normally she would have protested being knocked out but, drugged or not, troubled sleep was coming quick and she was far too tired to fight the nurse.

Her head dropped as she looked down at her pale legs. Without looking at the nurse she reached her hand out to grab the cup with the pills. The nurse handed it to her. Ann managed to throw her head back and swallow the pills all in one motion. There was no need for the water so the nurse placed the gown on the bed beside her and left the room.

She stood up, slipped out of her own night gown and into the blue hospital issued digs. She then lay back down and stared at the yellow stain. Before long her eyes closed and she could feel herself being carried away by a tide of a million tears. The wind was carried by the sound of the defeated cry which rang loudly in her ears. Soon she was drifting out to the ocean of sleep with no shores anywhere to be seen. Somewhere in the distance a radio could be heard over the waves of all her tears, and was playing a song she didn't recognize at all but felt strangely familiar,

"I'm just a bird on a wire,

watching each day just drift away

as all the young faced children walk by

 never noticing me at all.

 Baby you have flown beyond my reach.

But still I've stayed for that one last moment to find you

 in those depths too far down for me to go

 if I ever want to see the sun again."

Instead of swimming on into any direction, Ann let herself be carried away by the waves away from a single boat that was there to save her. The reel changed and she found herself racing in her go-cart back out in Suffolk county, against a number of faceless drivers. Her happiest moments were when she was flying along at ever accelerating speeds. The faster she went the better off it made her feel as if she was outracing all the demons who haunted her for far too long.

There was the mother who wished Ann was a boy and only loved her out of obligation while drowning herself and all reminders of her dead husband in wine and depression. And her brother the prince of the family who could do no wrong. His shadow shown so thick over her, it eclipsed her name even from herself sometimes. There would be nights when she was sixteen where Ann would leave the house for days with the latest boyfriend. When she returned no one seemed to notice she was ever gone.

There was her friend with MS who loved her but for whom she felt only kindness. And all those boyfriends, every one of them who came, lied, or she lied to them and left. Even though she never owned a motorcycle herself, she loved having boyfriends who did, feeling the vibration and power between her thighs and the wind against her skin. So as she raced around the track the events of the night before were miles behind her but yet somehow still seemed to be all too present.

It was then that she realized it wasn't the demons but her name as well as herself that she wanted to outrace and leave behind but they both always caught up to her sooner or later. In the end the greatest demons of all were those mornings she prayed would never come. For they illuminated all of her wishes and dreams which she had before the age of sixteen and have yellowed like old newspapers which will go left unread, only to litter the doorless, windowless room of everything she had hoped to forget.

Yet she still raced on as a growing rage enveloped her, the gun of this rage was always pointed inward. Ann thought herself a coward for not doing what she was sure needed to be done before the next morning came rolling in. It was this failure to escape a life which had long become a prison of her own that made her sleeping lips mouth the words, "you're such a fuckin' coward."

There was no parole for this sentence which she never asked for, only the hope of escape. A far off voice broke through into the dream as if it was God's voice, "Why did you let them knock you out with those pills?" But there was no answer. With every lap there felt no end to the speeds she could reach and for a moment the demons were nowhere to be seen. The anger broke and some light shine through, but only for a moment.

Ann kept gaining speed as the weight of gravity started pushing down on her. All the lights became a blur until she didn't see the other drivers at all. The sound of the passing wind grew silent, the kind of silence known only to the deaf or the dead. But still she went faster and laughed a lunatic's laugh. For she was beyond the reach of all those men who used her for her money or seemed to move themselves into her apartment or endlessly lied to her. She wondered if she had loved any of them. Oh how proud she was for having never been someone's wife; having never been owned or claimed ownership over anyone else. She took pride in this decision, often explaining to all her friends "This is one of the few good choices I made in my life."

Soon there were no drivers at all as the silence was replaced by the sound of waves crashing down into the waters of eternal midnight's endless sea. As she gained speed her laughter became more jubilant for she seemed to outrace those mornings she prayed would never come. She prayed to a god she neither believed in nor if he had been real surely must have forgotten her name. She had grown too used to dwelling in those tiers too far below for any angel in heaven to reach if they ever wished to see the light again. Besides he was not allowed to pass through the heavy metal door to the ward. So it really didn't matter now if he existed all. Even one's name had to be left at that door before entering. For the lifers, when they were called for their meds, their names became nothing more than a word they responded to, much like a cat or a dog. But soon the laughter stopped and the morning caught up to her and as it did the turns soon grew more narrow with each rising and falling of the sun until every turn became a hairpin turn and there was no room for error.

Ann woke with a startle. As quiet as the hallway was when she had fallen asleep it was noisy with feet shuffling back and forth, along with echoing voices. The squeak of the porter's cart which would stop every few seconds then start once more was coming closer to her room. Sitting in the bed across from her was a heavyset stranger with a short blond haircut. She was sitting back against a well-worn pillow, one leg crossed on top of the other reading a book with no print on the cover. The woman somehow sensed that she was being stared at and looked over at Ann,

"Oh hey you're finally awake."

"What's going on out there? What's the problem?"

"Its dinner time they always start at five o clock on the dot. They think that routine is what we need while we're in here. Personally I think that if we don't have a routine in our everyday lives how the hell is it going to help us here?"

Ann smiled halfheartedly at the stranger's last remark since it was her own strange routine that landed her in the wards to begin with. She did not answer, just sat up and swung her legs over the side of the bed. She just stared at her feet with an expressionless face. The stranger glanced at Ann then looked back to her book.

"My name is Janet by the way."

Ann looked up again and was able to show some sense of life in her face somehow. Her eyebrows pointed up at the corners.

"Ann."

Janet sat up in her bed to sit cross-legged. She was about to ask Ann why she was there but the death in her eyes told the whole story. They were not unlike a town crier ringing his bell in the dark and otherwise empty streets of a long forgotten city. The news was always flowing out of pale and desperate lips but no one ever seemed to be around to hear it and the unseen ears that were there were always deaf.

"I know you didn't ask but..."

Before she could finish the sound of the squeaking of the orderly's cart stopped in front of their room. The strangely pale nurse soon walked into the room with a tray on her arm. She looked at Janet with a cold stare. Janet, as if following some unheard order, stood up and walked over to grab her tray. The nurse turned back to the doorway where the orderly handed her a second tray. She turned to Ann who stood up and walked across the room grabbed her tray in obedient fashion and back to her bed. On the tray was a thin piece of chicken smothered in a thick gravy smelling like cheap microwavable meal, mashed potatoes and overcooked green beans. Last was a formless mound of apple cobbler and a container of fruit juice. The nurse left the room and the sound of the wheels once again moved on.

Ann stirred the meat in the gravy as the guilt of the night before started bumbling up in her throat. She felt the tears swelling up once again in her eyes. She looked up to see if Janet was watching her but her new roommate was too busy wolfing down her food.

"Man it's like watching a prisoner on death row devouring his last meal", Ann thought. She wiped her eyes with the back of the blue gown's sleeve.

Ann began slowly eating the apple cobbler feeling sickened by the sight of the meat. The guilt only grew larger until Ann swore that she was going to have another breakdown there and then if she couldn't put her mind onto something else.

"What were you going to tell me before the nurse came in?"

Janet looked up half startled as if she forgot someone else was in the room with her.

"What?"

"Before the nurse came in you said you wanted to tell me something."

"Oh yeah, I was going tell you why I'm here if you're interested in hearing it. But you don't need to if you don't want to. I understand. I was just trying to make conversation."

"Well it's up to you if you want to tell me. I'll certainly listen."

Janet put her spoon down on the tray, grabbed a napkin and wiped her face.

"I grew up in a really devout Catholic family, baptisms, went to church and confession every Sunday. The neighborhood priest marked our foreheads every Ash Wednesday. You know that kind of thing. When my brother and I were younger we played along with the whole thing, even started believing in some of it after a while. But when I was sixteen, I started getting a crush on this girl who sat next to me in class. I tried to get over it by sleeping with a lot of guys you know?"

"But nothing worked so I started hanging with this girl after school until I tried to kiss her. The bitch jumped up with disgust and ran out the door of my bedroom. I was humiliated. Well her parents told my parents next thing I know, I'm being taken to South Oaks for a mental evaluation. This is 1981 don't forget. When they refused to take me. Some stupid fuckin priest came in to try to 'counsel me out of my sickness.' This lasted for about a year when I left home and moved into my own place."

"I worked at some shit jobs until I got some grant money and went to school to study psychology. While I was there I found a girlfriend who I moved in with for about ten years. I started drinking heavily back then, especially when visiting my folks. Of course I could never bring my girlfriend over to meet them. But to make a long story short, I confessed my relationship to them. My family disowned me there and then, and I drank every day after that. My partner couldn't take it anymore so she threw me out. Fast forward to about three weeks ago I got a call from my brother, that my dad just died and he thought I ought to know. And you know what that little bastard told me? He said that the family would prefer it if I didn't show up to the funeral. Can you imagine that? I started to feel so guilty for everything I'd done to them which really put me into a tailspin. My partner now got really concerned by my outbursts and the fact I was never sober. I had cut back some years ago. I just kept crying, I want to die. She told me to stop or she would call 911. I told her if she did I would knock her out and showed her my fist but she knew I could never bring myself around to do it. So she called and here I am." Janet's voice hardened as she uttered those last words "and here I am."

Janet picked up her spoon without saying another word and started eating, her hand visibly shaking. Tears began running down her cheeks as the veneer of being in control began to fall away. She threw her spoon down on the tray and put her face in her hands and began to weep softly. As Ann stood to try and console her roommate the unusually pale nurse walked in announcing that supper time was indeed over and it was time to collect the trays. She turned to Janet who was still crying in her hands, gave her a glance of contempt then walked out. Hearing her footsteps fade down the hall, Janet lifted her head and wiped her eyes.

"At least I'm off the bottle here." She attempted a smile but she wound up only looking more defeated. "I haven't even thought of that stuff since I've been in here."

She then grew silent. Without a word both Ann and Janet walked out of the room and into the day room.

In the halls the echoes of human voices seemed to come from no particular direction. All the faces passing Ann were unfamiliar. Some moved towards the day room while others moved in the other direction. Still others seemed to move in no real direction at all. Some of these faces looked at Ann as they passed while others simply stared at the floor. One thin Hispanic girl passed with a sinister smile, looking straight into Ann's eyes but said nothing. The doors that lined the hall were either wide open or ajar. In one room, a heavy set black woman lay on her bed curled in the fetal position with one eye swollen shut while the other stared at the doorway vacantly seeing nothing. Her mouth slowly formed letters and words but said nothing audible.

"Her name is Margret. She came in yesterday night around the same time you did. Word has it that she is a prostitute and junkie. Her pimp beat her up for some reason according to the nurses but it's all only rumors around here," Janet stated solemnly.

Overhead a voice rang out of a loud speaker, "Ok guys, it's that time! Time for meds. Also I need to see Ann Horn in the nurse's office." Janet pointed down the hall to indicate the direction of the office, "straight down the hall. Just look for the long line. Most of the guys line up long before the announcement is even made."

Ann walked down the hall, past the Day Room and found the long line. A nervous and emaciated black kid who shook uncontrollably was speaking to a Swedish looking boy standing behind him, "They better give me my meds soon or I'm gonna kick that metal door down. Either the door is going to break or my leg is…"

Behind the last person in line a door stood open. Ann walked over to see if that was in fact where she was supposed to be. Inside three plastic chairs were placed side by side against the far wall. An older nurse was in the middle seat with a clip board and paperwork on her lap. The nurse looked up then she then smiled warmly at Ann. The woman's warmth also showed in her eyes and seemed genuine unlike the doctor's from the early morning interview. The nurse waved for Ann to come inside and take a seat. Ann walked in slowly and sat in the seat to the left of the nurse. The two greeted each other with a hand shake as the nurse continued to smile.

"Hello Ms. Horn, I'm Nurse Lynn. We need to go over a few things."

The warmth in her voice while seeming sincere somehow came off as a con, as noticeable as a shell game. It was impossible to know where the con began and ended but Ann was sure that the grandmother sitting beside her was going by a script.

"I spoke about you to the doctor a few minutes ago. We went over your medication protocol."

The smile and friendly look vanished from the nurse's face, replaced by a serious stare, though the warmth was still present in her voice.

"First, it says here in your records that you were placed on medication after your last visit to the hospital. Is that correct?"

"Yes that's true but I stopped taking them a long time ago."

"Why?"

"Because I hated the way they made me feel. I started walking around all day like a zombie and started to feel nothing at all."

"Well the doctor insists that we put you on 60 milligrams of the meds while you are here."

As if on cue of some well-planned act performed night after night, Ann's semi regular psychiatrist strolled into the nurse's station with a troubled look on her face. She then both greeted Ann and the nurse then sat in the seat to the right.

Ann just looked at her, stunned, but did not voice any objections.

"Sorry it took me so long to get here. I came as soon as I could. Bcv I've been really busy lately."

Without looking up from Ann's records, the nurse explained, "I was just going over with Ann the meds we would like to try with her."

Ann felt her body begin to stiffen and her defenses were now at full strength again.

"I told you I'm not taking any of those goddam drugs I'm not going to walk around like some zombie."

The words slid out of a clenched jaw and tightly balled fists.

"Look Ms. Horn, if you don't take these meds we will need to hold you indefinitely. Obviously we can't strap you down unless you're a threat to yourself or the staff while you're here, but the doctors can make your exit from this place very difficult. We can't let you leave while you're in this state" the nurse stated trying to keep the motherly tone.

Ann looked over at the nurse with a knowing grin. She was in her mind already walking out the metal door while the doctors and nurses watched helplessly, knowing the seventy three hours was up. And she was free to go home then her final destination. Her doctor looked over to Ann with concern in her eyes. She spoke softly with a bit of a quiver in her voice.

"Look Ann if you don't start to cooperate soon I will have to write a letter to the head doctor recommending that you should be kept here until you're on some sort of protocol. If these drugs don't work for you, you know other drug combinations can be tried. If you don't cooperate it will be very hard for you to get out of here even after your seventy three hours are over."

Ann now felt herself finding it hard to breathe as if she was an animal trapped in a net and as she struggled to free herself, the net seemed to only tighten. She began to feel that every breath became an effort.

"Don't I have a say in this? I'm not going to have these drugs forced on me! I'm leaving after my time here is up. I don't care anymore. You can't keep me here against my will! This is just a fuckin' hospital, not a prison! I'm only staying now because I have to - but after that I'm gone! Why don't you let me go home now! I promise I'll be fine. Just let me go! Please! Please!"

The doctor stood up in a moment of frustration but made sure not to raise her voice, "You have to calm down. We're not your enemies here. We didn't make you swallow those pills. We're just trying to help you figure this out so hopefully it doesn't happen again."

The nurse now spoke with the cold of the institution in her voice and all pretense of friendliness fallen away, stating flatly. "Listen - the head doctor can keep you here as long as he sees fit and that includes after the seventy three hours you seem to cling to for some reason."

The rope tightened further. Ann's fists were now clenched so tight that small red pools started dripping from her palms on to her gown. Her jaw was like that of a trap but the words that came through gasps were able to escape.

"Ok goddammit! You won! If you want to beat me, uncle, uncle already. I can't take much more of this."

Tears started to stream down her face. She looked down at her feet and started to cry like a defeated child. The nurse stood up and walked over to grab two cups sitting on a counter top near a sink. She then turned and stood in front of Ann handing her first the cup with the pills. Ann put her head back and dropped the meds into her mouth. Then the water.

"Ok open your mouth. Lift your tongue. Ok. Pull your left cheek. Now right."

It took almost no time for her head to feel light and off balance. Her hands began to relax. The nurse quickly ran over the cupboard and grabbed bandages and tape to wrap up Ann's now bleeding palms. After she was finished, Ann stood up,

"Can I leave now?"

"Sure."

Ann walked out and headed towards the day room. She could hear her doctor and the nurse speaking behind her. Their voices became muffled behind the closed door. But soon their voices gave way to the loud roar from the television set. When she reached the day room Ann noticed for the first time that it was much larger than she thought it was. The shroud of sleep must have hidden so much of this room behind some unidentifiable shadow. Off to the right of the room the television sat on a wooden stand. A small two-person couch along with some chairs created a half circle around the set. Three long tables were placed off to the left near a shelf with board games and playing cards. Two older men were playing chess at one of the tables while at another, a thin youngish girl was taunting another one around the same age.

The assailant just kept repeating "Why won't you tell me? Go ahead tell me. What, are you scared? Tell me. Come on you little bitch tell me…"

The other girl who was just as pale as the strange nurse who delivered the meals, just sat there with her hands covering her ears and her eyes closed tightly crying,

"No, no stop it. Leave me alone! Stop it! Leave me alone you bitch! Why won't you leave me alone! Fuck off!"

A nurses came over to break them up. She pulled the bully aside and spoke in the same comforting voice as the workers who spoke with Ann.

Ann walked over to the TV area. The couch and seats were all occupied. Janet was sitting near Alice on the couch. Alice seemed to be paying no attention to the set but stared off into space.

"Pull up a seat from one of them tables back there," A large heavyset black woman, whose head was shaved and scarred, suggested with only faint interest in her voice. Ann just walked over to one of the tables sat down and threw her head back and closed her eyes, listening to the television. The news was on featuring a story about a serial killer out on Long Island leaving the dismembered bodies of prostitutes by the waters of Sands Point.

Suddenly Ann could feel herself being watched. She didn't open her eyes or bother to lift her head.

"You got a quata now lady?"

"No."

"But I want a quuuata."

Ann finally lifted her head and opened her eyes. Alice was standing there crest fallen.

"I have no pockets and all my money is at home so please stop asking me."

"Ohh-kayyy." Alice walked out of the day room and down the hall towards the bedrooms.

Ann leaned her head back once more and felt the wards, both doctor and nurses and patients alike, fall millions of miles away. The buzzing from the tube lights filled her ears and suddenly she saw herself being put into a box and shoved into an incinerator. "I'm the luckiest one of all" Ann said to no one at all with no irony in her voice, into the great void of sleep. Feeling herself fall further into this dream she wished would never end, Ann felt her leg kick involuntarily which brought her back to the day room. She looked over to the couch again, the guilt swelled in Ann's chest and throat for being short with the strange woman but instead of apologizing to the woman, she migrated to the now open spot on the couch next to Janet. Janet turned to her with some surprise,

"Oh hey you're back. What took you so long at the nurse's office?"

"They want to put me on medication which I hate taking. I tried to explain to her that I walk around like a zombie all day. It's horrible to be walking around not being able to feel anything. I'd rather feel terrible than nothing. Then my therapist showed up which freaked me out. I should probably have handled things better I guess and not have yelled at them. But it's better than feeling like prisoner."

"You shouldn't make too much trouble for them. It's better not to be noticed or even remembered in this place. The more you stick out the more they will be inclined to label you a trouble maker and make it really difficult to be released. It's best to just disappear into the background or play along with them. Just take their pills while you're here, and your release will be almost automatic. That's unless they deem you too dangerous for the outside world, or to yourself. Christ what happened to your hand?"

"Oh I dug my finger nails a little too deep into my palms which drew a little blood. Nothing serious. I took the meds. I already feel light headed."

An older woman whose feet barely could touch the floor while sitting in her seat next to the television and whose back was bent so far over, leaning back became impossible, turned to the women, with a finger to her lips, "Sssshhhhhhhh. Shut the hell up!"

Turning to the senior, the African American woman furrowed her brow taking on a motherly role, "Ruthie you can't speak to people like that. This aint yo home here. Those girls can talk if they want to."

Ruthie turned to her with a twisted face and shot back, "If they want to talk let them go to their rooms. This is the only time I get to watch the news. I've already missed the last story. We should have the right to not be disturbed by noise."

"Noise? There is noise all the time here. All the hallways have noise all the fuckin' time. Voices, shoes, all the time! Goes on all the time even during bed time! All the time. Nurses and patients all the time, talkin' so loud! I haven't slept in a week so don't tell me about noise! And the buzzing from those goddam tube lights. Bzzzzzzzzzzzzzzzzzzzz! Leave it alone Ruthie."

Ruthie shrunk back like a scolded child with hurt eyes but without saying a word. She turned back to the television set. Ann and Janet looked at each other and started laughing, the laughter of two kids who discovered each other for the first time.

"These two do this all the time. They have this back and forth every single night."

Ann looked over to one of the windows but only saw the back of one of the lucky ones. There was no use in trying to look past the figure's back, out onto the world she was a part of just the day before but now sat as just another one of the forgotten ones. Everyone on the floor, both patient and staff alike have all been part of that outside world at one point or another. Inside the ward, they all lived a different world, one with a different legal apparatus. Extreme behavior was your ticket to stay as long as it wasn't too extreme, then off you would go, either strapped to your bed or escorted to one of the "quiet rooms." It was a world where if you were on twenty-four hour suicide watch, the law was to find the head nurse on staff every time you had to take a piss. That nurse would stand outside the stall to wait for you. This was the world where time had no meaning outside of meal time, med time and bed time. But there was one more important time that they all looked forward to. That was to see the doctor so he can evaluate you and if you were lucky, he'd give you your walking papers. The noises of wandering ghosts continued to echo in the hallways, as the incessant buzzing of the lights would forever continue to remind everyone there how much they were truly on the outside while calling the world behind the heavy metal door, home. Ann could feel herself growing tired again and turned back to the television to finish watching the seven o'clock news.

The Art of Escape

Do you still wonder
now that you've been washed out
into fate's unforgiving seas
while you were sentenced to a life
you swore was in the wrong body?
Living in the wrong body is a natural crime.
The price,
to live with a heart pressed against
the third rail.
This is caring too much
for
anyone who sends all your true loves reeling
into an explosive mind
where each morning sets off tiny detonators
causing explosions
of your fit
and fury
casting off the last burning embers
of your brilliant hatred
which you shaped into a rope
used in your finest
and final art.
You should have built a dividing wall
of pills
between your east and west
between the morning that owns us all
and the movie.
The one in your head
where you were always going to cast yourself
as that tragic loser following a fool's dream.
You should have realized that we all
have the plans of dull and frightened apes
who live with the debt of living with the drudgery
of carrying a name of the cheated
like a self-shaped cross down Willis Avenue.
We have never truly left the lonely forest
hunting for coffee and music

while believing there is a home
beyond those gray seas of your plans
beyond the music
beyond your name which you successfully stripped away
at last
and the cats who still wait for you at Jeannine's.

Did you really think
that all that was going to be left behind
was solitary confinement
where white roses bloom in the garden
at your feet?
In the Orient
white is the color of death
after all.

Was your plan of escape
to sink into this ocean's
desperate floors
or be carried away
to nowhere at all?
For these waters
will never carry you back home
now that you made sure
that your escape was not
left to chance.
For here there are no shores
or docks
or port cities with their rat eat rat spirit
or disjointed legal apparatuses
which
always points towards punishment of
the sleepless.

You should have known that the gray seas
of all your final plans has been painted
on the otherwise empty canvass of your
eternal sleep.
Even the mariners have sailed on
the artic winds born of your final breath.
Ghosts do grow tired of their own smell
in ruin
and became homesick.
The map home which burned in their hearts
bright as a street lamp at midnight
has turned to lightless ash.
And the way home is shrouded in rumor.

Even Ulysses grew tired of being out to sea
where all rumors
become ghosts of what
once
was.
And once you've been gone for far too long
then all old lovers will cease looking for
you
from over the horizon
sooner
or later.
You should have realized
we are all beginners in the game of the cheated.
It is
after all the loser's dance
in an effort to find the right
step
to navigate
through
the latest
undertow.

2
My own confession
I wish there was life that far out
then perhaps you could reach me by phone.
Never collect.
Could you imagine the bill?
Still
AT&T would send a collector to settle that debt.
Maybe you could send a letter
or smoke signals
from across the seas.

About the Author

Matthew Abuelo is a writer, professional blogger and award winning poet best known for his observations on life in modern day New York. Born in Manhasset in 1975 to a father enlisted in the military, he and his family traveled throughout most of his childhood, living in army bases across the United States and Germany. After an early stint as a counselor for special needs children, Mr Abuelo began focusing more attention on his writing, developing his skills beyond poetry, to other genres including fiction and journalism. As an activist he helped organize the StrapHanger's campaign to fight for public transportation in Nassau County in the 1990's, has been involved in various campaigns within the peace movement after the invasion of Iraq and Afghanistan and has worked as an affordable housing advocate in New York City. Living in an SRO on the upper west side inspired him to write about his friends and neighbors, the remnants of bohemian New York, struggling to survive in an increasingly hostile and antagonistic world.

His previous book *The News Factory: Notes from a Dying City* was published by Plain View Press in 2012. His two earlier books, *Organic Hotels* and *Last American Roar,* are available on lulu.com. A former journalist for the online news site Examiner.com, Mr. Abuelo currently writes for the Times Square Chronicles, a bi-monthly publication based in Hell's Kitchen.